A Long High Whistle

DAVID BIESPIEL was born in 1964 in Oklahoma and grew up in Harris County, Texas, in Houston. He is the author of five books of poetry, most recently *Charming Gardeners* and *The Book of Men and Women*, which was named one of the Best Books of the Year by the Poetry Foundation and received the Stafford/Hall Award for Poetry, and a book on creativity, *Every Writer Has a Thousand Faces*. He is the editor of the Everyman's Library edition of *Poems of the American South* and *Long Journey: Contemporary Northwest Poets*, which received the Pacific Northwest Booksellers Award. He writes the Poetry Wire column for *The Rumpus* and is a member of the board of directors of the National Book Critics Circle. Among his honors are a National Endowment for the Arts Fellowship in Literature, a Wallace Stegner Fellowship, and a Lannan Fellowship. Since 1999 he has been president of the Attic Institute of Arts and Letters. He lives in Portland, Oregon, with his family.

A Long High Whistle

Selected Columns on Poetry

David Biespiel

ANTILEVER

ANTILEVER PRESS
www.antilever.org

ISBN 978-1-938308-10-9
Library of Congress Control Number: 2014953394

First Antilever edition, 2015

0 1 2 3 4 5 6 7 8 9

For Christian Wiman

Contents

From the Past to Here

Theories of Thumb

Affirmation

And your very flesh shall be a great poem.
—Walt Whitman

Preface

Thrill at the Triumphs

I BELIEVE THAT MOST PEOPLE have little trouble reading a poem, that most people like poetry, that most people crave the pure pleasure of poems, and that most people want a poem that's not too obvious. Human beings admire mastery. We enjoy hearing an extremely talented musician play difficult music. We love watching an elite athlete—like a world-class diver nailing a high-degree-of-difficulty twisting and somersaulting dive with no more splash than a teardrop.

And we thrill at the triumphs of the poet who, like a sculptor, transforms the rough marble of everyday language into a sculptured poem of human aspiration.

Mastery arouses us because doing something difficult is hard.

In late 2002, *Oregonian* books editor Jeff Baker and I met in Portland to bandy around the idea of a monthly poetry column, in lieu of conventional poetry reviews, in the Sunday books section of the state's major newspaper. I came armed with what I hoped was an apt metaphor about poetry and difficulty. In particular—and because I knew that prior to being the paper's books editor Jeff had once been a sports reporter—I opted for a sports metaphor.

"I see myself as being, you know, like John Madden, the football color commentary guy," I said. "Anyone can follow the game but John Madden's experience brings you closer to the complex game beneath the game. He brings you closer both to the game and to the sport."

I went on in this fashion, though I needn't have. Because we both understood that just as John Madden shows viewers the Xs and Os of each play, what went well, what broke down, and just as he covers the history of the formations, who the players and coaches are and what he thinks matters most about the past, present, and future of the sport of football, and just as he brings his values about the art and practice of football, and just as he models watching football in a reliable, enjoyable, and insightful manner, my intention with a poetry column was to be like the chalkboard talk for what poetry is and how it works, to reflect upon what I think matters most for readers and writers of poetry.

I needn't have worried. Jeff Baker already wanted to expand coverage of poetry in the books section. He was actively commissioning reviews of new collections and had also started a feature to publish original poems each week. Few, if any, newspaper books editors have been a better friend to the poets than Jeff Baker, whose editorial generosity to me was offered with expertise, good sense, and a quiet directness. Following that lunch meeting began a monthly ritual that lasted from January 2003 to the fall of 2013, in which I would send Jeff a short commentary, essay, or reflection on the art of poetry, and would receive in reply a salutary, "Thanks, David."

Readers responded more volubly.

Some took the reflections and the lines of poetry to heart. A woman once called my house to say that she was so delighted by Muriel Rukeyser's "In Her Burning"—a poem about an old woman's randiness—that she was going to bring it to her book group. "The ladies will love it!"

Others said they pinned up the columns on their refrigerators. Many teachers wrote to say they posted the columns and poem on the corkboards in their classrooms. I often noticed them reposted online.

One Saturday afternoon at a local park, a regular reader thrust Robert Frost's "To Earthward" into my hands at our sons' fourth grade soccer game. The boys had played on the same team since kindergarten, and they would continue playing together through high school. There was a strange cultural peculiarity going on in that moment in southeast Portland on the sidelines of the soccer field—as other parents were shouting at kids to kick and chase the ball, she was waving her rumpled copy of the poem at me and demanding, "Could Frost be this dark?"

I answered her in my next piece.

The complaints piled up, too. One reader tried to convince me that poetry didn't deserve such attention—even monthly—declaring, "Only schoolmarmish, gray-haired biddies care about poetry."

I took that personally.

Gray-haired? Not yet, pal.

Schoolmarmish? OK, well, you got me there.

Another reader really let me have it, and I quote: "Why don't you ever introduce something by Billy Collins, Ted Kooser, Naomi Shihab Nye, William Stafford, Sharon Olds, or Maya Angelou. Poets that don't make me work."

I see his point. And his sensibility, too. If only Modernism had never taken place.

And yet his passion for those particular poets deeply underestimates both their talents and the historical importance of the conversational style. My poetry column, at least, was intended as an offering of what I hope are uncommon reflections about poetry, and not as a presentation of individual poems by specific poets. I mean, I realize now how many poets who mean the world to me—Czeslaw Milosz, above all, who has been a north star, and W. S. Merwin, Yehuda Amichai, and others—I just didn't get to. Even in the preparation of this book I have left out a couple dozen or so columns with poems I'm enormously fond of.

To illustrate my ideas about reading and writing poetry, I drew from poems that are longstanding masterpieces, forgotten beauties, and recently published gems. These reflections provide what I hope is a warm invitation to the art of poetry. I've tried to write in a plainspoken, conversational way and have tried to help readers make connections among the different styles and movements in poetry and understand how they fit together. I haven't hesitated to make aesthetic judgments, but I've done so, I hope, in order to invite you to come to your own conclusions.

Like a lifeguard letting you know the water is safe—to abandon the John Madden metaphor—I saw myself as the guy who says that you'll be OK diving right into a poem. Because just as you listen to music on your own or watch films on your own or read history on your own, reading poetry is something you most certainly can do on your own.

I've found it helpful, when reading poems, to have a handful of expectations in mind. They give me a standard from which to evaluate poems, a standard I have revisited and revised many times over. As much as we profess to favor originality in art, it might be more accurate to say that we want originality not to be made out of nothing, but to be refashioned out of something—something real. The very act of refashioning from the real is what we notice as original. Only in the most rudimentary ways is a poem a straight imitation of experience. A poem is a refiguring of experience. It's an invention of a new experience. A poetic experience. And, as a reader, it becomes mine.

I see each poem as being tethered to its cultural predicament and its historical conditions. This is why, in addition to the physical geographic border of a specific language—French or English or Russian or Dutch or Arabic, and so on—we have national poetries with particular, peculiar, and predominant national literary dramas. Naturally, there are complicated cross-border dramas, too: English-speaking poets in the West Indies, French-speaking poets in Lebanon, Russian-speaking poets in Ukraine.

Paradoxically, little new happens in poetry. There's adaptation, there's distortion, there's refinement. It's easy enough to imagine a future poetic movement called the New Beats or the New Agrarians or the New Imagists. But "neo" is about resurgence and reinvention, about revival, about nourishing the present moment and paying homage to the past.

I say all this but it's not like I was born with these values about reading, writing, or writing about poems, poets, and poetry. I now know that writing for so many years about how poetry is created has helped me enormously to think through my ideas about the entirety of the art of poetry. It has been enormously humbling, too.

The first piece of prose I ever wrote about poetry in a daily newspaper was in 1989 for the Book World section of *The Washington Post*. Aggravated by what I took to be an insipid poetry review the *Post* had recently published, I wrote to the editor, Michael Dirda, to offer my services as a reviewer and pitched him on some new books.

This was audacious of me. I was twenty-five years old. I had been writing poems for only three years, ever since I'd resolved to hammer out my life as a poet. I had never written a book review before.

"How do I know you're not married to one of these people?" Dirda asked in a subsequent phone call before assigning, on speculation only, a roundup of five books different from the ones I'd proposed. These included new collections by Lucille Clifton, James Dickey, and Louise Glück. Thus my career writing about poetry in newspapers began. Years after I wrote those first reviews for the *Washington Post*—and later for the *New York Times* and the *San Francisco Chronicle,* as well as for literary quarterlies—Jeff Baker and I cooked up the idea of a newspaper column in the *Oregonian* about poetry. I leaped at the chance to shift my role from reviewer to columnist.

Though I can't say I aspired to become a newspaper poetry columnist. My primary interest is, has always been, the writing of poems. Writing prose about poetry, in my case at least (and this may be true for others), has sometimes helped to keep the silence between writing poems at bay and to help me, as I said before, think through my preoccupations about the art of poetry. Over time, to be fair, I've been grateful to have the column in the *Oregonian.* It's been like a piece of real estate in the literary neighborhood to return to with regularity where I can talk to a loyal readership about the art of poetry.

When I stepped down from writing the column, it was a private decision and one I'd been mulling for some time. After more than ten years and over a 120 columns, I wanted to stop before I ran the risk, if I'd not done so already, of becoming dull, rote, or shrill. The decision had nothing to do with the *Oregonian* and only a little to do with the dwindling audience for daily newspapers or the diminished size of the books section. What I mean is, during my time, the newspaper allowed me complete freedom to write about poetry in a manner that interested me. Often I would be asked by readers if the newspaper ever forbade me from writing something or writing about any particular poet or insisted that I write about any particular poet. No, never, not once.

And so I hold with the view that newspapers and general interest publications ought to provide a discussion of poetry on the same pages as its coverage of civic, political, and sporting life. That the thrill of victory and the agony of defeat of both the world of sports and the world of the sonnet might exist side by side epitomizes the ideal, as William Carlos Williams once said, that "poetry is news that stays news."

Anyone can be a critic of new poetry. It's easy as burning down a barn. The vast majority of contemporary poetry of any era is usually forgettable and soon forgotten. The real challenge for a writer who writes about poetry is to try to figure out how a poem works the way it does and why it might defy the historical odds. Or at least to try to figure out how a poem defines—at the very least, characterizes and, at the very best, mythologizes—our time.

All the same, I'm uncertain about what influence a poetry column has. For me, the whole point of writing about poetry was less about trying, presumptuously or foolishly, to shape the literary landscape than to help stimulate some conversation about poems, poets, and poetry, and about the role these play in a modern civilized city and nation, and beyond. I've tried to explain, from my perspective, who poets are, how poems work, how the art got the way it is, and what all that might mean or lead to.

DB
Portland

Introduction

Mapping the Particulars

...glass views and begonia beds

When you're reading a poem, the process of following its patterns of emotional and metaphoric impulses is a lot like walking through the streets and alleys of a new city.

If you're like me, when you visit a new city, you're interested in figuring something out about the identity of the people and the distinctiveness of the city's history and contemporary spirit. I like to see how neighborhoods develop and emerge and connect to each other. I like to notice how people make their lives and livelihoods. I want to go to places only the local people know about, places not usually travelled by a sightseeing lug like myself. My interest is in the variety of cultural intersections—as best as I can infer them in so short an amount of time. I think of this as a form of cultural mapping.

Likewise, when I walk through a poem, I'm trying to map specific parts of its cultural, lyric, and metaphoric geographies and then locate where the parts intersect. The process of walking through a poem, as with visiting a new city, includes keeping an eye out for landmarks and sudden surprises, peculiar characters, and opportunities for memorable experiences. As with visiting a new city, the process of reading a poem taps into your ability to see, experience, and evaluate more than one thing at a time.

This process of noticing what is distinctive and what is connected is crucial to reading poetry.

I might put it another way. Remember the delicate acetate-papered pages in the back of your high school biology book with the Da Vinci-shaped human body spread-eagled like the letter X? You'd fold a thin page over the human figure to see the tributaries of the nervous system. Fold over another page, and you'd see the system of veins and arteries. Fold again, and you'd see the muscle system.

The process of overlaying the pages allows you to discover the content of the human body. It can be the same with reading a poem. "The content of a poem," Stanley Plumly once said, "includes the ways that all the things in a poem connect, not just its narrative—because there's never just one narrative in a poem."

When you come to read poetry, it's worth coming armed with a few questions. To begin with, it's worth asking of a poem, "Poem, what are your multiple narratives?"

Plot is one, for sure. There's also the narrative of a poem's music—that's the linkage of sound and sense in the poem. Then there's the narrative of a poem's diction. Also, the narrative of its emotions. And behind these, there's the narrative—the imprint—of the poet's mind.

And there are the narratives of argument and feeling, focus and digression, voice and personality, self and mask, private journey and public inheritance.

Of the many ways to describe a poem, there are four particularly useful ones: lyric, narrative, ode, and meditation. Poems of a certain length—under a hundred lines, I mean—will typically have some combination of these four elements. They'll have intense emotional and figurative language (lyric), a sequence of events (narrative), praise for what's observed (ode), and a conceptual reconsideration of the subject (meditation).

When we say that a poem is a narrative poem, we're describing the dominant element in that poem—that the plot, drama, sequence of events, and storyline make up the major experience of the poem, or that those factors are more dominant, at least, than the other major elements of lyric, ode, and meditation. But we're not saying that the poem doesn't have any of the other elements. Just that the narrative element is the most consequential.

You can't "get" all of that in just one quick reading of a poem. That's why you first walk through a poem while mapping its particulars. Walking through might begin with evaluating the title. Consider Anne Stevenson's "The Fish Are All Sick." What could this title tell you even before you read the poem? It says the fish are "all" sick. Really? All of them? This strikes me as being either a silly exaggeration or a way to talk about an internal crisis. I admit that I like to question a title's outlook before I read a poem. Take, for example, Walt Whitman's "Song of Myself." I want to ask, somewhat cheekily, "What other songs are there, Walt?"

When you poke at a title like this, like poking a stick into a fire, you let yourself fidget with how the poem might illustrate, character-ize, make a metaphor, or even undercut its apparent intentions. At the same time, you allow the poem to challenge your own developing assumptions.

Next, you might walk through and map both the first line and the last line of the poem in combination. Here are the first and last lines from "The Fish Are All Sick": "The fish are all sick, the great whales dead" and "And closing its grip, and closing its grip." What you might notice is the parallel rhythm in the two lines. When you're poking around like this you really have no idea what that rhythm means or suggests, or whether it means anything at all other than just offering rhythmic delight. But the rhythmic similarity is there in the first and last lines, it is parallel, and so it can raise in your mind an interest in the very idea of parallel-ness as a subject in the poem. At the very least, it's a place of interest. I don't mean to suggest that you should force a reading onto the poem. Instead, devising questions before you settle into actually reading a poem enlivens your mind to that poem's ambiguities and possibilities. When you're reading a poem, you can't behave like a potted plant.

Same goes for applying a little arithmetic to a poem. Count the total number of lines in the poem—because shorter poems work differently from longer poems. Shorter poems typically demand that their endings be intensely resonant. Shorter poems open up like an inverted cone into sudden rushes of meaning or feeling. On the other hand, longer poems tend to have more concrete sorts of resolutions.

I'm oversimplifying.

But a good starting point for measuring how the lengths of poems might create meaning goes something like this: shorter poems want to feel long, and longer poems want to feel short.

Stevenson's poem adds up to a dozen lines with two uneven stan-zas. The poem is probably going to invite you to anticipate a sudden overflowing of meaning at the end.

Below, you can see if it does: but, before you do, check out the last
words of every line in the poem before reading it. And also browse
the poem in a cursory way on the hunt for obvious metaphors. As you
perform these two bits of mapping, ask more questions, such as "Why
are these specific words at the ends of the lines and not others?" and
"What is potentially significant about this or that metaphor?" and
"Why is metaphor X at the beginning of the poem while metaphor Y
is near the end, and how do they relate?" Here is the poem:

> The fish are all sick, the great whales dead,
> The villages stranded in stone on the coast,
> Ornamental, like pearls on the fringe of a coat.
> Sea men who knew what the ocean did,
> Turned their low houses away from the surf.
> But new men, who come to be rural and safe,
> Add big glass views and begonia beds.
>
> Water keeps to itself.
> White lip after lip.
> Curls to a close on the littered beach.
> Something is sicker and blacker than fish.
> And closing its grip, and closing its grip.

What do you make now of the last words in each line: *dead, coast, coat,
did, surf, safe, beds, itself, lip, beach, fish, grip*? The contrast between *dead*
and *safe* has my attention, for sure.

Once you begin to read a poem, you don't need to try to get
everything in the first go round—in the same way you don't try to
understand everything about a painting at first glance or even a city
at first glance. What you don't get immediately you can just graze
past, like running your hand through your hair to get the tangles out.
When I first walk through a poem, I'm mostly keeping an eye out for
the prevailing metaphors to see whether they give me any pleasure. I
leave it at that until I read the poem over again.

At this point, from the early process of poking around and walking
through "The Fish Are All Sick," what do we know? We know the
poem is about fish. And we might suspect the fish are metaphors
for something human—because poems, after all, are about the great

story of human life far more often than they are about the great story of marine life.

Last, mapping the particulars means going back to the beginning of the poem and starting the whole process again, though this time, and in subsequent readings, you have the advantage of having actually read the poem so you know more of what to expect. You can focus on things you skimmed over before. You're now aware of some of the poem's routes and byways better than you were the first time. The process is like knowing how to get back to your hotel after a few excursions well enough that you can now look into the nooks and crannies along the way with more experienced eyes. This is how walking through a poem, followed by reading it closely, deepens your experience and lets ambiguities emerge.

In the end, it's not just you reading the poem, but the poem reading you. Even reading itself. This strategy of walking through a poem asks you to listen to the poet's mind and the language of her imaginative life, even actual life. Because contrary to the current literary fluff about the dissolution of the author, I feel it's self-evident that the life of the poet is intrinsic to the life of the poem.

And so mapping the particulars of a poem and reading in this fashion can go a long way to establishing a communion between you and the poet who has offered you her poem.

What Does It Mean?

It is impossible to say just what I mean!

If You Have to Ask

Once a reader wrote to say that I often use the expression "lyric poetry," but what does it mean?

It's a great question, though part of me wants to respond as Louis Armstrong did when asked to define jazz: If you have to ask, you'll never know.

Ancient poetry was oral, often chanted, and arose out of the pleasure human beings discovered when combining words into a meaningful sequence and using the melismatic rhythms of one's voice to impart feelings. The traditional definition of lyric is that of a poem composed to be sung by a solitary singer, with musical accompaniment, on a single theme, and as an expression of personal feeling.

This singing or chanting led to poetical schemes to improve clarity, such as common melodies, refrains, rounds, and rhymes. What we've come to think of as forms—sonnets, for instance—are really abstractions. They became useful when poetry was eventually written instead of memorized, and they were tests of a poet's mastery of imagination and language.

Remember the Scotsman Robert Burns's lyric?

> O my luve's like a red, red rose
> That's newly sprung in June:
> O my luve's like the melodie,
> That's sweetly play'd in tune.

To read it from a purely technical stance is to see that it contains a 4/3 metrical rhythm—four accented beats in the first and third lines tethered to the three accented beats in the second and fourth lines, something like "o MY luve's LIKE a RED, red ROSE / That's NEWly SPRUNG in JUNE."

It's a rhythm Cole Porter could have written—and often did:

> Your fetching physique is hardly unique,
> You're mentally not so hot;
> You'll never win laurels because of your morals,
> But I'll tell you what you've got

The soft stress of a sound followed by a hard stress of a sound—that's the root rhythm of lyric poetry in English. And yet only a few people a hundred miles outside of Edinburgh can probably sing the customary melody that goes with "A Red, Red Rose," and Porter's "You've Got That Thing" is scored and accompanied by piano.

So here's the important difference since about the sixteenth century: modern lyric poetry isn't sung and doesn't require musical accompaniment. Instead, lyric poetry is more like rhythmic speaking. The accompaniment is silence.

It may be best to think of the phrase lyric poetry as a metaphor, one that contains the idea of the ancient poetic singer but isn't a singer exactly. And still, while there is an implied social contract, think of it as a solitary speaker. Or, as the late Donald Justice once put it, lyric poetry is "a kind of virtual speech. It becomes that by imitating speech which might actually be spoken on some occasion."

Donald Justice's "Bus Stop" is just this sort of lyric poem. Set in San Francisco's Potrero Hill where the poet once lived, the poem contains musical qualities, such as repetition, that you might associate with song:

> Lights are burning
> In quiet rooms
> Where lives go on
> Resembling ours.
>
> The quiet lives
> That follow us—
> These lives we lead
> But do not own—
>
> Stand in the rain
> So quietly

When we are gone,
So quietly...

And the last bus
Comes letting dark
Umbrellas out—
Black flowers, black flowers.

And lives go on.
And lives go on
Like sudden lights
At street corners

Or like the lights
In quiet rooms
Left on for hours,
Burning, burning.

The multilayered repetition of the words *lights, burning, rooms, quiet, quietly, lives, black flowers, go on* creates a chiming cadence (add to that the rhyme and distant imbedding of *ours* into *hours*). The effect of the echo seems to reinforce the speaker's isolation.

But don't take it from me. Take it from Justice. "Bus Stop" is "unmistakably a lyric poem," he wrote, "which by its nature could stand quite a lot of *sound* [his italics]...I wanted anything which had to do with the sound or music to come in very simply and in a completely natural way, almost as though by chance...If rhymes showed up—and they did—they were to remain casual, not part of a deliberate scheme...Repetition—a type of rhyme itself—turned out to play a larger role in the sound of the poem...The effect came to resemble what you get in a poem with multiple refrains, or, more fancifully, when several bells are set swinging at different timings."

Sound is just one quality of lyric poetry. More could be said about lyric poetry's use of metaphor or its general brevity and sensuous imagery—and it raises the question, thinking of my earlier example, of why does it give us pleasure to imagine love as a red, red rose?

It gives us pleasure because lyric poetry is a literary presentation that isolates human experience and connects the solitary voice of the poet to anyone willing to listen.

To Disenchant and
Disintoxicate

Visiting my mother one time I was poking around the bookshelves and came across an anthology from my childhood, *A Little Treasury of Great Poetry*, edited by Oscar Williams and published in 1947. The copy is a hardbound first edition, bought for $3.50, and I remember reading it often during high school and as my constant companion on trips home from college.

A poetry anthology is like a museum exhibition, and Oscar Williams was a tireless curator. He was the originator of the *Little Treasury* series and was one of the first to produce record albums of poets reading their own work—the Def Poetry Jam of its day.

Great Poetry contains some five hundred poems dating back to the thirteenth century and includes the trademark of a Williams anthology, a gallery of poets' portraits, beginning with reverential images of Chaucer and Shakespeare, then marching through the centuries—Sidney, Pope, Keats, Browning, Dickinson, and so on—until concluding with a puffy-cheeked, boozy-eyed snapshot of Dylan Thomas. How many hours a young poet could stare at those portraits and dream of being among them I don't wish to say. The book is divided by a queer assortment of themes, such as Up in the Airy Mountain, Imperfections of Man, Beauty of Women, Inconstancy, and the like.

An early favorite of mine from the Despair and Suffering section was W. H. Auden's "Musée des Beaux Arts," which Auden wrote in the late 1930s. Born in 1907 in York, England, Auden was deft at using varied poetic forms in everyday, conversational language. The poem begins:

About suffering they were never wrong,
The Old Masters: how well they understood
Its human position; how it takes place
While someone else is eating or opening a window or just
    walking dully along;
How, when the aged are reverently, passionately waiting
For the miraculous birth, there always must be
Children who did not specially want it to happen, skating
On a pond at the edge of the wood:

And what the masters know about human experience is that, despite
catastrophe, we must move on, carry on, and even quickly learn to
forget:

They never forgot
That even the dreadful martyrdom must run its course
Anyhow in a corner, some untidy spot
Where the dogs go on with their doggy life and the torturer's
    horse
Scratches its innocent behind on a tree.

There's a case to be made that the poem might do well to stop here.
The point is made. Despite the suffering of existence, despite the pain
of living, we must endure with our "doggy life." We must not become
intoxicated by the dissonances of living.

I'm sure I was attracted to a poem like this one because it illustrates
what Auden elsewhere calls poetry's ulterior purpose of truth-telling,
namely "to disenchant and disintoxicate." With this concept sim-
mering on the poem's back burner, the poem makes its startling turn
toward an essential human characteristic that so many poems animate
and dramatize: we endure. Here's the conclusion:

In Brueghel's *Icarus*, for instance: how everything turns away
Quite leisurely from the disaster; the ploughman may
Have heard the splash, the forsaken cry,
But for him it was not an important failure; the sun shone
As it had to on the white legs disappearing into the green
Water; and the expensive delicate ship that must have seen
Something amazing, a boy falling out of the sky,
Had somewhere to get to and sailed calmly on.

Here's where the title makes its mark, referring to the Museum of Fine Arts in Brussels. The poem is based on Peter Brueghel's sixteenth-century painting, "The Fall of Icarus," about the Greek myth in which Icarus flies too close to the sun, burns his wings, and plunges to the sea to his death amid a bustling scene of commerce and daily life.

In two nonchalant sentences, the poem conveys our "human position" of indifference toward suffering—about which the Old Masters are "never wrong." Icarus's death is an extraordinary "disaster," as is the martyrdom in the first stanza, but it has little effect on the living world. And, while suffering is ever-present, we still live our lives and, like that expensive ship at the end of the poem, we must sail "calmly on."

Crossing the Frontiers of Language

At its best, a translation crosses frontiers of language and imagination and holds up what is universal and universally mysterious about being human.

But the translation from one language to another—from Portuguese to English, say—is never an exact replica. It is, instead, a rendition, a cultural reembodiment. The translator rides the edge between humility and risk, submitting to the original even while working to change it.

Sometimes the risk can be fatal: the novelist Salman Rushdie's Italian translator of *The Satanic Verses* was stabbed, and his Japanese translator was stabbed to death.

Once the frontiers are crossed, the boundaries of the new language can even be extended. Rendered from Latin translations of Greek translations of the Hebrew original, the King James Bible, for instance, became a seedbed for the rhythms and cadences of our English poetic tradition. William Shakespeare's debt to translations of Italian narratives is enormous—and his enrichment is ours. Try to imagine a world of poetry in English without Dante, Baudelaire, Basho, Rilke, Akhmatova, Neruda, Milosz—and the list could go on—had these poets not been translated. What a limited spiritual reach we would have without them.

Born in rural Portugal near the Spanish border in 1923, Eugenio de Andrade published his first book at the age of nineteen and is one of Portugal's most popular and most decorated poets. In the translations of Alexis Levitan, he comes across as a poet grounded in the fundamental emotions of human existence, as in the opening sections of "Still Life with Fruit":

1

The morning blood of raspberries
chooses the whiteness of linen to love.

2

Morning filled with sparklings and sweetness
settles its purest face upon the apple.

3

In the orange, the sun and moon
are sleeping hand in hand.

The terrestrial is brought in sync with the celestial: raspberries and love, morning and sweetness, the human body and the cosmos. As with so many lyric poems, we are invited to care deeply about the classical elements of air, water, earth, and fire. Here are the last sections of the poem:

4

Each grape knows by heart
the names of all of summer's days.

5

In pomegranates, this I love—
the stillness in the center of the flame.

Thriving on sensual imagery and metaphor, these sections climb the "highest boughs," as de Andrade writes in another poem, in order to sing the "ecstasy of day" as a morning song of magnified perception. In each of its five image-laden parts, "Still Life with Fruit" locates the "stillness in the center" of what is seen and brims with the language of passionate awareness—blood, sweetness, hand in hand, heart, summer, love.

Isn't the theme of love pivotal to this poem, too? It's the word that ends the opening couplet, and it's the only verb attached to the poem's speaker ("In pomegranates, this I love—") in the only moment in which the speaker enters the poem.

That's why lyric poetry is so often dedicated to a sense of occasion. In "Still Life with Fruit," for instance, the poem's occasion—a still life—is borrowed from another art form, painting.

That, in itself, is another form of translation.

Mishmash of High and Low

Like an ever-growing, dynamic beast, the English language devours foreign roots and foreign words. Take a line like this one from August Kleinzahler—"Garbage scows move slowly down the estuary"—and you'll find etymological sources from the French (garbage), Dutch (scows), and Latin (estuary).

New words come into being almost daily or at least new arrays of old words (as in *pork bellies*, *mainframes*, and *airport*). Every industry has its gibberish, every generation its jargon, every region its twang. The English language confounds: how is it that *fat chance* and *slim chance* mean the same thing?

Poets delight in playing host to these lexical and fossilized metamorphoses because, in the end, all that a poet has to work with are the words on the page. How a poet intimately fashions his language—whether cooking it or leaving it raw, as Robert Lowell more or less put it—defines his poetics and style. To write poetry in American English is to negotiate a hodgepodge of diction—rural and urban, commercial and political, technological, regional, statistical, psychological, ethnic, slang, and Strunk and White.

This mishmash of high and low speech is a hallmark of August Kleinzahler's poems. He was born in 1949 in New Jersey, went to school in Manhattan, then Wisconsin, then Vancouver, British Columbia. In Vancouver, he studied with the terrific British poet Basil Bunting.

One thing Bunting seems to have passed along is the importance of working with language that is distinct, something Bunting accomplishes in his masterpiece, "Briggflatts." For any poet to be original, Bunting once said, that poet must "bear the peculiar features of their own language" in the forefront of their mind.

Another influence on Kleinzahler is William Carlos Williams, from whose sequence "January Suite" he gets the title for one of his books, *The Strange Hours Travelers Keep*. Here is the opening of Kleinzahler's title poem:

> The markets never rest
> Always they are somewhere in agitation
> Pork bellies, titanium, winter wheat
> Electromagnetic ether peppered with photons
> Treasure spewing from Unisys A-15 J mainframes
> Across the firmament
> Soundlessly among the thunderheads and passenger jets
> As they make their nightlong journeys
> Across the oceans and steppes
>
> Nebulae, incandescent frog spawn of information
> Trembling in the claw of Scorpio
> Not an instant, then shooting away
> Like an enormous cloud of starlings

You might detect from these lines that Kleinzahler has inherited Williams's urban sensibility and deft feel for the idiomatic. But where Williams profited by the environs of Patterson, New Jersey, Kleinzahler's cityscape is often his longtime hometown of San Francisco. The result of these influences is poetry that delights in the elasticity and diversity of America's lyric language.

The poem continues:

> Garbage scows move slowly down the estuary
> The lights of the airport pulse in morning darkness
> Food trucks, propane, tortured hearts
> The reticent epistemologist parks
> Gets out, checks the curb, reparks
> Thunder of jets
> Peristalsis of great capitals
>
> How pretty in her tartan scarf
> Her ruminative frown
> Ambiguity and Reason

Locked in a slow, ferocious tango
Of *if not, why not*

Doesn't a line like "The lights of the airport pulse in morning darkness" illustrate urban vibrancy? Also, doesn't it show Kleinzahler's cynical playfulness by undercutting the tradition of Classical rosy-fingered sunrises? Then a line like "Nebulae, incandescent frog spawn of information" shows the way a poet can maneuver around diverse diction. It's this juggle of idioms that any poet who writes in American English—and who wants to write something distinct and new—must master.

Incantation

When the British poet Thom Gunn died in April 2004, at the age of seventy-four, the news left me feeling unhinged in a way I didn't expect.

Many poets begin their efforts as writers in the ecstatic thrall of writing itself. Later, they hunker down to the important work of systematically reading all the poetry they can find. For me, this effort was the reverse. I was reading and reading poems long before I began trying to peck some out in my early twenties and also before I began to structure my entire life around writing and thinking about poetry.

During that incubation, canonical poets mattered the world to me, especially Keats and Wordsworth, Whitman, Dickinson, and Yeats. Among living poets, Thom Gunn ranked near the top of my list. After Gunn's death I realized that there had never been a time when he wasn't a central influence on my conception of poetry's ambition. Namely, to tell the truth with artistic control, good humor, intensity, and what he once called a "trusting search for the correct incantation."

Thom Gunn was born in Gravesend, England, in 1929, and he studied at Cambridge. He fell in love with an American, and the two men moved to San Francisco in 1954. His ticket to America was a year of study at Stanford University as a recipient of the university's poetry scholarship, now known as the Stegner Fellowship. He would remain mostly in San Francisco ("England is my parent," he once remarked, but "San Francisco is my lover"), teach regularly at the University of California, and publish a dozen books of poetry.

Gunn is the only poet I know of who draws on Renaissance and Augustan metrical rhythms—think John Donne and Andrew Marvell—in order to write about motorcycle toughs, LSD, and free love. He juxtaposes tradition with an impulsive feel for the glorified, raw moments of being, for comradely affection, and for cool, metaphysical contemplation. The entire poem "Listening to Jefferson Airplane (in the Polo Grounds, Golden Gate Park)" from the 1970s goes: "The music comes and goes on the wind, / Comes and goes on the brain." And here's another couplet-length poem from the early 1990s, "Jamesian," as in the novelist Henry James, that goes: "Their relationship consisted / In discussing if it existed." These two poems represent a signature gesture in Gunn's poetry. He teases out the contradictions of his emotions.

I met Thom in 1994, after he'd seen a review I'd written of one his books. I was living in San Francisco then, and he invited me to his home for coffee. I saw him last in January 2004, when we read together in Berkeley and shared a ride back to the city. He was graceful and clarifying as a man and as a poet, and a poem like "The Hug" typifies his demeanor:

> It was your birthday, we had drunk and dined
>> Half of the night with our old friend
>>> Who'd showed us in the end
>> To a bed I reached in one drunk stride.
>>> Already I lay snug,
> And drowsy with the wine dozed on one side.
>
> I dozed, I slept. My sleep broke on a hug,
>> Suddenly, from behind,
> In which the full lengths of our bodies pressed:
>> Your instep to my heel,
> My shoulder-blades against your chest.
> It was not sex, but I could feel
> The whole strength of your body set,
>> Or braced, to mine,
>> And locking me to you
> As if we were still twenty-two
> When our grand passion had not yet
>> Become familial.
> My quick sleep had deleted all
> Of intervening time and place.
>> I only knew
> The stay of your secure firm dry embrace.

All the inclinations of lyric utterance are in play here, including the initiation of an occasion ("It was your birthday"), the imposition of an altered state of affection ("I dozed, I slept. My sleep broke on a hug"), the clarification of understanding existence ("It was not sex, but I could feel"), and the realization of a permanent moment in time ("I only knew / The stay"). The poem invites you to clarify the meaning grace, as it is manifest in both love and time.

I remain attentive to the influence of great poets and try to glean from them what the future of a life in poetry holds. That night in the taxi, what Thom Gunn told me was unexpected. He said he'd stopped writing poetry four years earlier. "I'm retired now," is how he put it. "Now," he went on to say, "in the afternoon I sit and read a book, with a glass of wine, and the cat jumps into my lap. Then we both take a nap."

Thus, the clarified lesson that silence is essential to poetry's music, too.

To Witness and to Sing

I've always been leery of overtly political poetry. It's often bad poetry, poorly written, and not effective as political statement either.

Of the two kinds of political poetry, the first has never interested me. That's the poem written to persuade, convince, induce, or sway you to its political position, the kinds of poems designed to forward a partisan agenda. If, for instance, we already agree with the agenda (ethnic cleansing is bad, say), then we're just one of the choir being preached to. We might even say the poem is good, great, or terrific, but only because the poem proves we've been right all along.

If we disagree with the agenda—Rudyard Kipling, for instance, wrote poems in praise of colonialism—then aren't we right to call the poem simply propaganda?

In the end, overtly partisan poetry is hardly persuasive as poetry. It's political speech. And I would defend it as such. I support the right of anyone to the freedom to write a bad poem. Yes, a bad poem, because by subordinating poetry to politics, overtly political poetry scorns the language and is an enemy of the imagination.

Still, one thing a poem can do is free the self from constraint. That's the second kind of political poem, where the politics are as much a part of the poem as any other part, such as the imagery, lineation, metaphor, variation, rhythm, dissonance, harmony, diction, and so on.

You can see the effects of mixing the lyric with the civic in Yeats's little poem "Politics." Every election cycle I find myself drawn to it for its ability to enlighten and distract. Yeats wrote it during the 1930s, with World War II on the horizon, after serving as an anti-Nationalist Senator in the Irish Parliament. His chief contribution in the Senate was overseeing the redesign of Irish coins.

How can I, that girl standing there,
My attention fix
On Roman or on Russian
Or on Spanish politics?
Yet here's a travelled man that knows
What he talks about,
And there's a politician
That has read and thought,
And maybe what they say is true
Of war and war's alarms,
But O that I were young again
And held her in my arms!

What we look for in a poem—or at least what I look for—is surprise and strangeness. I want to see the untranslatable translated into language and form ("O that I were young again"). I want to be delighted. I want the poem to reveal complexities—say, of suffering ("Of war and war's alarms") and joy ("And held her in my arms!"). I want the poem to record, to remain unforgiving, to forgive. I want a poem that witnesses and sings.

With that in mind, you can see how resistant Yeats's "Politics" is to being political. But what can be more political, more biased and subjective, than yearning for love to save the world? Politics, the dubious philosopher Groucho Marx once said, is "the art of looking for trouble, finding it everywhere, diagnosing it incorrectly, and applying the wrong remedies."

"We make out of the quarrel with others, rhetoric," Yeats once remarked, thinking about political life, "but of the quarrel with our-selves, [we make] poetry."

Election days come and go. The decision about the future of a city, state, or country is often burdensome, true. But for one fleeting moment it can help to "fix" our attention on something else. Our problems will be there when we get back. By looking away, we might see clearly where we are and where we dream of going.

This Is the Meaning of It

I've always loved Robert Frost's proclamation: "I'm only a poet when I'm writing a poem."

First, it emasculates the pretentious concept of the life of the poet, where the poet is considered a species apart from everyone else. It also describes the act of writing poems: how a poet lets his imagination get seized by an idea, image, sound, or word and then fashions that experience into a new verbal shape, what we call a poem.

The serious poet, I hear Frost saying, commits equally to both the act and the results of writing. To borrow a phrase from W. S. Di Piero, the poet's job is to "look to see" in order to remake experiences afresh.

And not just that. The poet's job is to invent a real documentation with that music. If things go well, the poet says through his poem, I'm alive, I'm human, and this is the meaning of it.

Seen in these terms, W. S. Di Piero's cinematic single-sentence poem, "The View From Here," authenticates the poet's burden of witnessing our interconnected society through the subject of a family sleeping in a car:

It's not hard to find them any night, sleeping under autumn stars,
the nameless, swept away or under, asleep or dozy, car heater off,
a gentle poisoned wind blowing through the window, the toddler
kicks and growls like a dog dreaming, the older son's closed eyes
twitch as if he can't chase or flee those pictures fast enough,
and the parents, too big and hot, how every hour or so they wake,
touch, nudge to make room in their early model front seat,
fresh water to last the night, chips and Snickers, diapers, gum,
celebrity gossip rags, cover sheets for the children,

breathing inside sullen steel blued by moonlight, under a trestle
or interstate, in an off-season stadium lot, untended campground
or back street, or parked there behind a strip mall's Dumpster pod,
just like last night, times before and to come, if we look to see,
then to imagine the tribes together, junkers amassed like tortoises,
in an abandoned drive-in, windows steamy, voices and grunts
as we walk past the secrets of the day jobbers, housecleaners,
nannies, pickers, and busboys camouflaged among us, on their way
to greater goods, dreaming of how we stand here watching them.

Like William Blake's "London," Di Piero's "The View From Here"
is a poetic documentary. It presents, distills, understands, and em-
pathizes. Poetry, Di Piero once said elsewhere, is an "attempt to fuse
and discriminate . . . to blend into words the unsorted particulars of
experience, and to make words not report the conflict but enact it."

That's what poetry can give us. We might, for example, see our
lives as separate from the downtrodden family in the car but at the
same time we realize that's not entirely the case either ("It's not hard
to find them . . . "). Because by witnessing them at the moment they're
dreaming of us ("dreaming of how we stand here watching them"),
we're implicated in their struggle—no, our struggle, as so many poems
attest—to live with dignity.

Occasion of the Non-occasion

One summer night, about 3am, I was awakened by street noise out-side the window—some kids shooting off fireworks on the sidewalk. Turning on the porch light scared them off, and I climbed back into bed. As I drifted back to sleep, I began to listen closely to the steady, easy breathing rhythm from my son in the next room, leaving me amazed again by what a calming, familiar, and reassuring sound that is.

Lying there, I began to think of a new poem that I'd read a week or so earlier by Adrienne Rich, "Memorize This." Here's the opening:

> Love for twenty-six years, you can't stop
> A withered petunia's crisp   the bud sticky   both are dark
> The flower engulfed in its own purple   So common nothing
>   like it
> The old woodstove gone to the dump
> Sun plunges through the new skylight
> This morning's clouds piled like autumn in Massachusetts
> This afternoon's far-flung like the Mojave
> Night melts one body into another
> One drives fast the other maps a route
> Thought new it becomes familiar
> From thirteen years back maybe
> One oils the hinges one edges the knives
> One loses an earring the other finds it
> One says I'd rather make love
> Than go to the Greek Festival
> The other, I agree.

I don't know exactly why this poem came to mind and not some other poem. I don't know exactly how any poem comes to mind in a moment like that. Or in any moment.

What I know is, some entrancing bits of remembered language that have wonderfully fetched, secured, and defined an experience suddenly connects to my own experience, in this case, the nightly ritual of bed and sleep. Was it phrases like "both are dark" or "Night melts one body into another" that I couldn't shake for their juxtaposition of lucid mystery? Don't know. For whatever reason, without effort, Rich's poem came to mind at that moment in the night.

I believe it's common for us to turn to poems in this way.

Poetry confirms, broadens, and signifies the fine moments of our mortality. That's what was happening that night in my bed, and that's what happens in the second part of the poem, too:

> Take a strand of your hair
> on my fingers let it fall
> across the pillow   lift to my nostrils
> inhale your body entire
>
> Sleeping with you after
> weeks apart   how normal
> yet   after midnight
> to turn and slide my arm
> along your thigh
> drawn up in sleep
> what delicate amaze

We use poems to record our elated feelings of falling in love or to soften the bruises of breaking up, to celebrate the newly born and to honor the recently dead. Whether using intricate or simple words, received or invented forms, the best poetry heightens experience ("what delicate amaze") through the use of our common language. The language of poetry is one of the things we share as human beings—within our own and across the dialects of the world.

What I mean is, if poetry did not exist for even a single day that would be the day it gets invented.

And yet this poem or that poem is not about an occasion per se, but about a totality of experience that eventually isolates a moment. It is, to use Stanley Plumly's expression, about the occasion of the non-occasion, one of lyric poetry's most important spots of time. Whether it's noticing a "strand" of hair or turning to "slide my arm / along your thigh," Rich intensifies the typically unnoticed. Or, to invert a line from the poem, Rich transforms the "familiar" into something "new." She asks to be imprinted ("Memorize This") by what she understands to be true from her discovery.

Adrienne Rich is probably best known for writing political poetry and for writing about women's rights. Few contemporary poets have written as convincingly as she has on the subject of the poet's public role. Over some five decades of publishing poetry and essays, and especially since the 1970s, her writing helped to define the women's movement and influenced public discourse about the politics of culture, gender, language, race, and sexuality.

Thinking now about waking that night to the sound of my son's breathing, I think of something else Rich has written, a single sentence from her great essay, "When We Dead Awaken": "Until we can understand the assumptions in which we are drenched we cannot know ourselves." That's one role for poetry, too. Poetry connects individuals to each other and forms routes of communion—such as what is shared and passed on as a legacy between, well, a father to a son.

In other words, poetry's cause is the cause of human dignity. "Art," Adrienne Rich once wrote, "is our human birthright, our most powerful means of access to our own and another's experiences and imaginative life." A poem like "Memorize This" probes and enraptures the "delicate" experience of enduring love. Behind it is the authority of a poet who also knows that one role of the poet is to be amazed by the fact of our simply being alive.

One Kind of Knowledge

Occasionally I find myself steered into a conversation about poetry's perennially small audience compared with other arts, and why it is that poets don't target their work to expand that audience—the way, one person suggested to me, record companies do. I fear I'm being asked, why don't poets focus-group their poems to better reach a mass audience?

It's an interesting question. But could you imagine Emily Dickinson poll-testing her poems in some Victorian version of the sterile conference room? "You're going to have to standardize that syntax and punctuation, Miss Dickinson."

I don't think so.

Besides, poetry has never had an interest in being a mass art. It's barely even commoditized. True, there is an implied social contract between poet and—let's call it—listener, even if the poet often feels that hardly anyone is listening.

Here I'm reminded of Kenneth Rexroth's wisecrack: "I've had it with these cheap SOBs who claim they love poetry but never buy a book."

So who is the poet's audience?

A poet writes for what you might call the audience of one. A poem begins with the human voice as a solo sound—literally, I mean, the breathy or deep or what-have-you vibrations of the poet's actual vocal cords, as she uses the medium of language.

Next, the poem moves through the ears and eyes of a single reader until it finds a new sound in that reader's own voice. New sound and new meaning. Because it's the reader who speaks and interprets the poem into being when saying it out loud. The reader, after the poet, becomes the speaker and the consciousness of the poem.

As much as our relationship to reading a poem is intellectual, imaginative, and emotional, it's also intimately physical. A poet reaches her audience one reader at a time, one poem at a time, one voice at a time.

Muriel Rukeyser was a poet deeply concerned with poetry's audience and also deeply committed to writing poems that investigate what it means to live in a socially and politically complicated world, especially as a woman. "I write from the body," she once said, "a female body." Her poems demand that readers put their body in her place and be willing both to be challenged and to accept difficult truths.

Rukeyser was born in 1913 in New York City, published her first book, *Theory of Flight*, in 1935, and died in 1980. She was a single mother who published over fifteen books in her lifetime, was president of PEN (the international writer's union), was investigated during the McCarthy era because of her political activities and put under surveillance by the FBI, and went in protest to Barcelona during the Spanish Civil War and to Hanoi during the Vietnam War. She is one of America's most renowned poets. She's influenced every generation of poets that has followed her, including poets like Anne Sexton, Adrienne Rich, Sharon Olds, Marilyn Hacker, Ruth Stone, and Rita Dove.

On the subject of poetry's audience, she thought that most people fear poetry and don't let something so foreign as a poem enter their daily lives. And yet "Everywhere we are told," she once said, "that our human resources are all *to be used*, that our civilization itself means the uses of everything it has. But there is one *kind* of knowledge infinitely precious, time-resistant more than monuments, here to be passed between the generations in any way it may be: never to be used. And that is poetry."

"In Her Burning" is typical of her celebration of the carnal impulses of life that poetry is so exhilarated by. It begins:

> The randy old
> woman said
> Tickle me up
> I'll be
> dead very soon—

Nothing will
touch me then
but the clouds
of the sky
and the bone-
white light
of the moon
Touch me
before I go
down
among the bones

From this erotic zone of being, the lines reorient in time and space, demonstrating that there is a synchronicity between life's inner and outer experiences:

My dear one
alone
to the night—
I said
I know I know
But all I know
tonight
Is that the sun
and the moon
they burn
with the one
one light.

Wouldn't you say the poem argues that physical pleasure at any age and for any sex is as natural as the rising of the sun and the moon? And so Rukeyser concludes:

In her burning
signing
what does the
white moon say?
The moon says
The sun
is shining.

"In Her Burning" sketches the indispensability of human yearning. It helps define poetry's uses. If poetry is to be responsible to anything, surely it must speak about our flesh as it is—regularly hungry and continuously oscillating between "burning" and "shining."

That's how a poem transmits its ideas from one person to another. It's a communion of human voice to human voice, from vibration to vibration. The audience of one is receptive to the voice of another. And not just receptive, but immersed in that voice, with "the one / one light" that is the poet and the reader speaking together.

Lost to Words

Great poetry, the Italian poet Eugenio Montale once said, arises from a personal crisis of "discontent, of an inner emptiness which the achieved expression temporarily fills." As with these opening lines from the beginning of his poem "Salt," translated by Jamie McKendrick:

> We don't know if tomorrow has green pastures
> in mind for us to lie down in beside
> the ever-youthful patter of fresh water
> or if it means to plant us in some arid
> outback ugly valley of the shadow
> where dayspring's lost for good, interred beneath
> a lifetime of mistakes. We'll maybe wake up
> in foreign cities where the sun's a ghost,
> a figment of itself and angular
> starched consonants braid the tongue at its root
> so all sense of who we are is lost to words,
> and nothing that we know can be unraveled.
> Even then, some vestige of the sea,
> its plosive tide, its fretwork crests will surge
> inside our syllables, bronze like the chant of bees.

When you look at this passage, you can see that the act of writing poems contains an interesting paradox. The poet is just as often "lost to words," to quote a phrase from Montale, as he is at a loss for words.

Writing poetry is a process of both recovery and discovery. Born of some disturbance, the seizure of the poet's imagination becomes the weird beginnings of a poem. This could be a bodily pang or a stray image, even a mood. The feeling could arise from memory or dream, yearning, confusion, fear, anger, love, or contemplation. It's just a feeling, a consciousness, an absence of words, a loss for words.

The written poem develops when a poet translates his wordless feelings into language. That's what it means to be "lost to words." It means to be lost to and inside of language's tribal sources and contemporary charms. I suppose this is what William Wordsworth meant, too, when he says that language is the "incarnation of thought."

But the translation from sensation to poem is at best only a version of the original feeling—or a variation on it—that hopes to reveal the urgency of poetry.

What I'm getting at is that while a poet like Eugenio Montale believed that "nothing that we know can be unraveled," he also understood that poetry seeks to unravel what we know.

"The subject of my poetry (and I believe of all possible poetry)," Montale says elsewhere, "is the human condition considered in itself; not this or that historical event." Adding, we must have "the awareness, and the will, not to exchange the transitory for the essential."

Eugenio Montale was born in Genoa, in 1896, and died in 1981, six years after receiving the Nobel Prize for Literature. He served as an infantryman during World War I. He published his first book of poems, *Bones of the Cuttlefish*, in 1925. Living in Florence in the late 1930s, he refused to join the Fascist Party. For that act of civil disobedience he was dismissed from his job. He moved to Milan after World War II and devoted the rest of his life to writing poems, criticism, and translation.

An introspective poem like "Salt" exhibits Montale's operatic voice and impressionistic use of language. It exhibits the idea that a poem breaks through to discern what is below the surface of consciousness. Here's the ending of it:

> However far we've stumbled from the source
> a trace of the sea's voice will lodge in us
> as the sunlight somehow still abides in
> faded tufts that cling to bricks and kerbstones
> on half-cleared slums or bomb-sites left unbuilt.
> Then out of nowhere after years of silence
> the words we used, our unobstructed accents,
> will well up from the dark of childhood,

and once more on our lips we'll taste Greek salt.

This conclusion is a good illustration of a poet being both lost to words and at a loss for words. Where "Salt" opens with the phrase, "We don't know if tomorrow has green pastures" (which is to say, we don't know if it doesn't either), by the end of the experience, the poem embraces the unknown. Put differently, while the poem begins in anxious anticipation, even discontent about the future, it ends in the mixed consolations of the past—the briny "dark of childhood."

What does a poem do for us? A poem can change your life, yes, but it's also only a poem. As Montale wryly noted in his Nobel Lecture, poetry is an "absolutely useless product, but almost never harmful, and this is one of its claims to nobility."

Revere and Condemn

A poet's greatest fear is that she will flinch.

Whether addressing suffering or love, failure or success, life or death, war or peace: a poet wants—merely, only, absolutely—to be courageous in the face existence. And yet on the issue of war and peace the question is often asked: can poetry matter?

Well-known poets have been known to try to impact political events. Robert Lowell twice defied a US president. First with FDR, when Lowell declared himself a conscientious objector during World War II, becoming the first male in the Lowell family not to serve in the armed forces since the Revolution. Later, to protest Vietnam, Lowell refused an invitation from LBJ to speak at the White House.

Another example of a poet's political protest is that of Adrienne Rich. Outraged over the chronic racial and economic injustices in this country, Rich publicly refused to accept the 1997 National Medal of Arts from the Clinton administration.

The post-9/11 war in Iraq also provoked defiance from poets. Prior to the invasion, the Port Townsend editor and poet Sam Hamill gathered thousands of poems and delivered them to the White House to protest the imminent assault. To denounce the ongoing fighting in Iraq, Sharon Olds publicly challenged an American president when she refused an invitation to attend a White House lunch.

But what of it? The violence and the injustices were not stopped by a poet's protest. A government can betray its own soldiers in war, and yet I'm certain, as well, that poetry can do nothing about it. Ernest Hemingway was right when he said that it was once thought to be "sweet and fitting to die for one's country. But in modern war, there is nothing sweet or fitting in your dying. You die like a dog for no good reason."

For a poet, getting it right about war—inside the workings of a single poem, I mean—means finding a form and music that are necessary and insistent to the cause. It means facing war's dark ambiguities: that war is humanity's greatest crime (what Homer calls the "butchery of men"), that the soldier's honorable wish is to be honorable, and that a country may be conquering and wrong at the same time.

In the final analysis an enduring poem goes beyond politics and headlines.

When a poet writes a poem—about war or anything else—she writes as one voice singing for the human tribe. That voice must always be, as Marianne Moore says, "unfalsifying."

Marianne Moore's "Keeping Their World Large" is a response to a 1944 *Times* article the day after D-Day that read, "All too literally, their flesh and their spirit are our shield."

The poem begins:

> I should like to see that country's tiles, bedrooms,
> stone patios
>   and ancient wells: Rinaldo
> Caramonica's the cobbler's, Frank Sblendorio's
>   and Dominick Angelastro's country—
>   the grocer's, the iceman's, the dancer's—the
> beautiful Miss Damiano's; wisdom's
>
>   and all angels' Italy, this Christmas Day
> this Christmas Year,
>   A noiseless piano, an
> innocent war, the heart that can act against itself. Here,
>   each unlike and all alike, could
>   so many—stumbling, falling, multiplied
> till bodies lay as ground to walk on—
>
>   "If Christ and the apostles died in vain,
> I'll die in vain with them"
>   against this way of victory.
> That forest of white crosses!
>   My eyes won't close to it.

All laid aside like animals for sacrifice—
like Isaac on the mount,
      were their own sacrifice.

My speculation is that the word "shield" took Moore by surprise, and she entered the writing of her poem to see what "shield" might mean when put against the reality of the day's "sick scene."

Here's the conclusion:

    Marching to death, marching to life?
"Keeping their world large,"
      whose spirits and whose bodies
all too literally were our shield,
    are still our shield.

    They fought the enemy,
we fight fat living and self-pity.
      Shine, o shine,
    unfalsifying sun, on this sick scene.

These lines are an example of an unflinching strike against political and poetic complacency: "They fought the enemy, / we fight fat living." And, too, they invoke something patriotic that—without the low-hanging fruit of overused and overly symbolic language—a voice speaking for others must strive for in a poem.

It's hard now to call America's early twenty-first-century experience in Iraq a war in the traditional sense when compared with the army-on-army combat and carnage that was World War II. But call it what you will—invasion, street fight, struggle, war—it's hard to read Marianne Moore's poem and especially the last stanza about our country's "fat living" and not feel war's cruelties.

Since her death in 1972 in New York City at the age of eighty-four, Marianne Moore has been stuffed into a strange caricature—the baseball-loving poet, the spinster poet, the raconteur poet who was called on during the fifties by the Ford Motor Company to name one of their new cars. Her suggestions—"The Utopian Turtletop," "The Mongoose Civique"—are brilliant and crazy but ended up losing out to the "Edsel," which itself went bust.

A poem like "Keeping Their World Large" shows Moore seriously wrestling with poetry's highest ideals and pressures. To revere and to condemn, as well as to see what is, what will be, and what has been before. And to be certain that our "eyes won't close to it."

Limitless Solitude

Anticipating the arrival of Valentine's Day one year, I'd been thinking that one of the more dicey kinds of poems to write is the love poem.

A great deal of what we think of as love poetry is actually about heartbreak, and so a necessary emotion for a poet is pain, loneliness, and anguish. Not an uncommon emotional state for a poet, some may argue, but there it is.

Next, the poet more or less formalizes that distress into lines and stanzas, as the first-century BC Roman poet Catullus does in his classic two-line poem "Odi Et Amo":

> I hate and I love. Why is this, you ask?
> I don't know, but I'm in torment.

On the other hand—and often worse, for a reader, that is—is a love poem that blindly praises the beloved. This sort of mallet of emotions is about as sexy as a letter of recommendation.

Everyone knows that the mysteries of love—spiritual, carnal, first, new, old, absent, platonic, lost, fumbling—are central to human experience and have always been one of art's core subjects. So a love poem works best when it has a visceral, almost electric collision of energy running throughout. As with any fine poem, its language surprises us with a fresh unveiling. Let's call that a surge of emotion, imagery, and metaphor.

One master of the love poem is the Chilean Pablo Neruda (1904–1973). Neruda was born Neftali Ricardo Reyes Basoalto. His father disapproved of his interest in writing, so to avoid detection he adopted Neruda as his pen name. He became a protégé of Frederico

Garcia Lorca, wrote several dozen books, and was awarded the Nobel Prize in 1971.

A love poem wrestles with what Neruda calls our "limitless solitude." Here is the beginning of W. S. Merwin's translation of "Here I Love You":

> Here I love you.
> In the dark pines the wind disentangles itself.
> The moon glows like phosphorous on the vagrant waters.
> Days, all one kind, go chasing each other.
>
> The snow unfurls in dancing figures.
> A silver gull slips down from the west.
> Sometimes a sail. High, high stars.
>
> Oh the black cross of a ship.
> Alone.
> Sometimes I get up early and even my soul is wet.
> Far away the sea sounds and resounds.
> This is a port.

But Neruda also felt that one's solitude is not insurmountable. He believed that poetry can result in a form of communion: "Poetry is an action, ephemeral or solemn, in which there enter as equal partners solitude and solidarity, emotion and action, the nearness to oneself, the nearness to mankind and to the secret manifestations of nature."

When you read the rest of the poem, you can see how this idea of communion resolves:

> Here I love you.
>
> Here I love you and the horizon hides you in vain.
> I love you still among these cold things.
> Sometimes my kisses go on those heavy vessels
> that cross the sea towards no arrival.
> I see myself forgotten like those old anchors.
>
> The piers sadden when the afternoon moors there.
> My life grows tired, hungry to no purpose.

I love what I do not have. You are so far.
My loathing wrestles with the slow twilights.
But night comes and starts to sing to me.

The moon turns its clockwork dream.
The biggest stars look at me with your eyes.
And as I love you, the pines in the wind
want to sing your name with their leaves of wire.

Yes, love can sometimes hide among "cold things." Yes, it sometimes needs to be disentangled and unfurled. But, in the end, like a poem, love can also survive and sing. Love poetry strives for just this sort of ideal. To portray love's endurance, to give praise to love's essential place in the body and the spirit of human existence.

"Here I Love You," published when Neruda was just nineteen, is an expression of the love of "secret manifestations." That's one notion behind the grand idea that poetry is a limitless solitude communing with other limitless solitudes.

Atmosphere, Action, Control, and Coincidence

Every time I'm in Washington, D.C., I visit the National Gallery so that I can spend, if I have the time, upwards of an hour looking at Jackson Pollock's masterpiece, "Lavender Mist." It's one of my favorite paintings, a ten-foot canvas in scribbles and splatters with the flung paint thickening and thinning and thickening again in enigmatic depths—like the lights and darks of a galaxy. For me, the painting is less about spontaneity than it is discovery, a hallmark of artistic mastery.

As many times as I've thought about this painting—and always when I've been in its presence—it brings my imagination to a renewed understanding of expressive urgency. The mist of all that spattered paint may seem wild, even incoherent, to some. But all that movement coheres, too. All that color-saturated action, busy-ness, and apparent disorder is anchored to Pollock's astonishing achievement with movement and to what I think of as a painter's version of lyric improvisation and inventiveness.

That's what I was thinking the last time I was in the nation's capital. I look forward to seeing the painting again in the future because, as the poet Anthony Hecht once said, a "serious and durable work of art, whatever its medium, will make the sort of demands upon us that invite repeated experiences that will fail to exhaust the work."

I have often felt the same way about Hecht's poem, "A Hill," published in his 1967 book, *The Hard Hours*. It begins with a common experience of a tourist looking at his foreign surroundings:

In Italy, where this sort of thing can occur,
I had a vision once—though you understand
It was nothing at all like Dante's, or the visions of saints,
And perhaps not a vision at all. I was with some friends,
Picking my way through a warm sunlit piazza
In the early morning. A clear fretwork of shadows
From huge umbrellas littered the pavement and made
A sort of lucent shallows in which was moored
A small navy of carts. Books, coins, old maps,
Cheap landscapes and ugly religious prints
Were all on sale. The colors and noise
Like the flying hands were gestures of exultation,
So that even the bargaining
Rose to the ear like a voluble godliness.

Then the poem's sensuous clarity and laconic, orderly sense of apprehending the experience suddenly shift into the promised vision:

And then, when it happened, the noises suddenly stopped,
And it got darker; pushcarts and people dissolved
And even the great Farnese Palace itself
Was gone, for all its marble; in its place
Was a hill, mole-colored and bare. It was very cold,
Close to freezing, with a promise of snow.
The trees were like old ironwork gathered for scrap
Outside a factory wall. There was no wind,
And the only sound for a while was the little click
Of ice as it broke in the mud under my feet.
I saw a piece of ribbon snagged on a hedge,
But no other sign of life. And then I heard
What seemed the crack of a rifle. A hunter, I guessed;
At least I was not alone. But just after that
Came the soft and papery crash
Of a great branch somewhere unseen falling to earth.

Not much of a vision, really. Cold weather. Bare trees. Breaking ice. A ribbon, a gunshot, a falling branch "somewhere unseen falling to earth." How can you have a vision that is so, well, visionless? One of the virtues of poetry is to distract, to create disorder, to disrupt your expectations—though, to be fair, Hecht does warn us that his vision is hardly Dantesque.

When a poem encounters the extraordinary, it sets you up for a new atmosphere of understanding. It passes through a threshold from one reality, say, modern life, into another reality, the poetic life of invention, inspiration, and metaphor. There's little difference in ambition between Pollock's abstract expressionism and Hecht's concrete realism. And, in both cases, their vision must conclude with clarity and understanding:

> And that was all, except for the cold and silence
> That promised to last forever, like the hill.
>
> Then prices came through, and fingers, and I was restored
> To the sunlight and my friends. But for more than a week
> I was scared by the plain bitterness of what I had seen.
> All this happened about ten years ago,
> And it hasn't troubled me since, but at last, today,
> I remembered that hill; it lies just to the left
> Of the road north of Poughkeepsie; and as a boy
> I stood before it for hours in wintertime.

Once a poem has passed the threshold from the living to the imaginary, the poem must return again to the real world. So too with the poet. Like a hero on a quest, the poet must return from the realm of coincidence back into the former lived world of his community and daily affairs. And not just return. But return with fresh understanding of the realm of the imaginary and also the realm of the real.

In both its composition and representation, "A Hill" is plainly different from Pollock's "Lavender Mist," I know. But, surprisingly, I also find them similar in that both the painting and the poem are full of atmosphere and action, control and coincidence—four elements necessary for any artist serious about the relationship among the creative senses.

Hecht was born in 1923 and died in 2004. Serving in the Army in World War II, his division discovered the concentration camp at Flossenburg. The experience of liberating death camp prisoners—especially as Hecht was assigned to translate their statements—left him desperate to comprehend the immensity of inhumanity. Since he published his first book, *A Summer of Stones*, in 1954, Hecht's poetry, though not without its lighter touches, has been marked by a reticent, grave, and moral seriousness, one conditioned on an abiding trust in and need for formal precision.

"A Hill" is as relaxed and chaotic as it gets, formally, for Anthony Hecht. As many times as I've read "A Hill," the line "I remembered that hill; it lies just to the left" has never failed to move me. It suggests that the core experiences buried in the life of one's imagination are ever-present—"just to the left," in our consciousness. And, as with Pollock's "Lavender Mist," they are thickening and thinning, and awaiting discovery—and rediscovery.

To See the Invisible

Wallace Stevens once said that a poet is a "priest of the invisible," meaning, I suppose, that a poet—who is not a priest obviously but more like a conjurer—is astonished by all things, including by what is barely known or fleetingly known, by what is all but imperceptible or what is suddenly realized, and even by what is absent entirely. For Stevens, the poet is both a seer and a clarifier of meaning.

Thinking of poetry this way, I'm reminded of lines from Donald Justice's "Memory of a Porch: Miami, 1942," lines that concentrate on what is seen and what is not seen—though here seeing means listening:

> What I remember
> Is how the wind chime
> Commenced to stir
> As she spoke of her childhood,
>
> As though the simple
> Death of a pet cat,
> Buried with flowers,
>
> Had brought to the porch
> A rumor of storms
> Dying out over
> Some dark Atlantic.

Justice has an eye—and ear—for the presence of what is missing. It's as if he is able to detect "a rumor" of perception. Louise Glück possesses this skill and talent, as well. In her poems the invisible is often located in a psychological and spiritual place.

Born in 1943 in New York City, Glück writes autobiographical poems that typify the art of introspection. Her poems are austere and unflinching. It may seem uncharitable to call her writing merciless, but if you'll accept that as praise—and that's how I mean it—then that's what her writing is, especially when her poems are a projection of a self-lacerating mask of mind and heart.

A caution in this regard, however. Mere observation is insufficient for a poet. The "true in poetry," Glück once said, "is felt as insight," adding that insight "is very rare, but beside it other poems seem merely intelligent commentary." Poetic insight comes about through a poet's ability to see what exists, into what exists, nearly what exists, and beyond what exists. In short, to see the invisible.

For example, her poem "Telescope" is focused on just this sort of vision. It opens:

> There is a moment after you move your eye away
> when you forget where you are
> because you've been living, it seems,
> somewhere else, in the silence of the night sky.
>
> You've stopped being here in the world.
> You're in a different place,
> a place where human life has no meaning.
>
> You're not a creature in a body.
> You exist as the stars exist,
> participating in their stillness, their immensity.

Here the poem begins by turning away from its own occasion: "There is a moment after you move your eye away / when you forget where you are." Though poetry is often thought of as the art of memory, forgetting is sometimes also crucial for a poet, as the following lines argue next:

> Then you're in the world again.
> At night, on a cold hill,
> taking the telescope apart.

43

You realize afterward
not that the image is false
but the relation is false.

You see again how far away
each thing is from every other thing.

This poem's act of forgetting leads to a place, or passage, between what is known and unknown. For a poet, the occasion of forgetting calls forward another occasion, that of invention—"You've stopped being here in the world"—and leads toward inner discoveries.

And these places of discovery are the invisible geographies where a poet's mind can evolve and grow.

The art of writing poetry is also the art of mapping what is always present. Or, as Glück puts it at the turning point of "Telescope": "Then you're in the world again" where you must see "how far away / each thing is from every other thing."

Perfection of the Imagination

Often when we come to a translation of a poem into English, we know fairly certainly that we're reading an imperfect interpretation of the original, a strange mimic, or even what seems like an entirely different poem altogether.

Given the differing cultural and linguistic histories of any two languages, translators seldom attempt word-for-word renditions. Instead, translations are an aesthetic rendition that tries to get the poem to work in the new language. Readers would do well to remember that, at best, a translator weaves his consciousness into that of the author's. At worst, he ignores it.

Most of my experience with translation has been from another language into English. That is, if you don't count high school Latin examinations when I was required to sight-translate the Gettysburg Address into Ciceronian prose ("of the people, by the people, and for the people" hashed out as *ut populare et a populo et pro populo*). Which is to say, most of my experience with reading poetry in translation is reading from a language I don't know into one I do.

I was thinking of this in Italy once when I bought a bilingual English-to-Italian translation of John Keats's poems while visiting Keats's apartment in Rome at the foot of the Spanish Steps—where, in 1821 and at the age of twenty-five, he died of consumption. Though I know translations are a tricky business, I was totally caught off guard by Mario Roffi's English-to-Italian version of "Ode to a Nightingale," especially the last lines, which I'll quote in a moment.

The Nightingale Ode, which Keats wrote two years before he died, is one of the finest poems in our literature and a poem that has deeply influenced my own writing. In the poem, Keats describes listening to a nightingale sing its evening song and dreams of joining with it—bard with bird, as it were—through the purity of poetry and the imagination. But as the reverie ends, he realizes that he must return, after all, to the "weariness" and "fret" of daily living.

After the nightingale departs with the sunset, Keats responds to the dreaminess of the experience by asking:

> Was it a vision, or a waking dream?
> Fled is that music:—Do I wake or sleep?

The last question has always interested me, as it has centuries of readers. It's a question as much about the limits of the imagination as it is about the limits of the actual world. Keats's questions respond to the entire experience described in the poem. They also crystallize his feelings about his capability and desire to live in a world that cannot fully accommodate the perfection of the imagination.

Here is the poem:

> My heart aches, and a drowsy numbness pains
>   My sense, as though of hemlock I had drunk,
> Or emptied some dull opiate to the drains
>   One minute past, and Lethe-wards had sunk:
> 'Tis not through envy of thy happy lot,
>   But being too happy in thine happiness,—
>   That thou, light-winged Dryad of the trees
>   In some melodious plot
>   Of beechen green, and shadows numberless,
>   Singest of summer in full-throated ease.
>
> O, for a draught of vintage! that hath been
>   Cool'd a long age in the deep-delved earth,
> Tasting of Flora and the country green,
>   Dance, and Provençal song, and sunburnt mirth!
> O for a beaker full of the warm South,
>   Full of the true, the blushful Hippocrene,
>   With beaded bubbles winking at the brim,
>   And purple-stained mouth;
>   That I might drink, and leave the world unseen,
>   And with thee fade away into the forest dim:

Fade far away, dissolve, and quite forget
     What thou among the leaves hast never known,
The weariness, the fever, and the fret
     Here, where men sit and hear each other groan;
Where palsy shakes a few, sad, last gray hairs,
     Where youth grows pale, and spectre-thin, and dies;
          Where but to think is to be full of sorrow
               And leaden-eyed despairs,
     Where Beauty cannot keep her lustrous eyes,
          Or new Love pine at them beyond to-morrow.

Away! away! for I will fly to thee,
     Not charioted by Bacchus and his pards,
But on the viewless wings of Poesy,
     Though the dull brain perplexes and retards:
Already with thee! tender is the night,
     And haply the Queen-Moon is on her throne,
          Cluster'd around by all her starry Fays;
               But here there is no light,
     Save what from heaven is with the breezes blown
          Through verdurous glooms and winding mossy ways.

I cannot see what flowers are at my feet,
     Nor what soft incense hangs upon the boughs,
But, in embalmed darkness, guess each sweet
     Wherewith the seasonable month endows
The grass, the thicket, and the fruit-tree wild;
     White hawthorn, and the pastoral eglantine;
          Fast fading violets cover'd up in leaves;
               And mid-May's eldest child,
     The coming musk-rose, full of dewy wine,
          The murmurous haunt of flies on summer eves.

Darkling I listen; and, for many a time
     I have been half in love with easeful Death,
Call'd him soft names in many a mused rhyme,
     To take into the air my quiet breath;
Now more than ever seems it rich to die,

To cease upon the midnight with no pain,
  While thou art pouring forth thy soul abroad
    In such an ecstasy!
Still wouldst thou sing, and I have ears in vain—
  To thy high requiem become a sod.

Thou wast not born for death, immortal Bird!
  No hungry generations tread thee down;
The voice I hear this passing night was heard
  In ancient days by emperor and clown:
Perhaps the self-same song that found a path
  Through the sad heart of Ruth, when, sick for home,
    She stood in tears amid the alien corn;
      The same that oft-times hath
Charm'd magic casements, opening on the foam
  Of perilous seas, in faery lands forlorn.

Forlorn! the very word is like a bell
  To toll me back from thee to my sole self!
Adieu! the fancy cannot cheat so well
  As she is fam'd to do, deceiving elf.
Adieu! adieu! thy plaintive anthem fades
  Past the near meadows, over the still stream,
    Up the hill-side; and now 'tis buried deep
      In the next valley-glades:
  Was it a vision, or a waking dream?
    Fled is that music:—Do I wake or sleep?

That last question points Keats and all of us toward the future, for
sure—as if asking: Now what do I do? Do I wake? Do I sleep? And
which of these is real?

Once you know the poem, you will come to feel that Mario Roffi's
translation of the ending of the poem is striking and bizarre:

> Forse fu vissione
> o sogno ad occhi aperti? Sono sveglio
> o dormo? Quella musica è fuggita.

Which is: "Was it a vision / or a waking dream? Do I wake / or sleep?
That music is fled."

By reversing the last two items, Roffi's Italian version purges Keats's poem of its existential quandary about both the past and the future in the lived world. In Roffi's "Ode to a Nightingale," the poet responds to the first question—"Was it a vision or a waking dream?"—by immediately asking the second question (Keats delays the second question)—"Do I wake or sleep?" Then as the bird flies away, the poet in Roffi's version moves to speak in a minor key—"That music is fled." Posed at the very end of the poem, this last doleful sentiment is not just anticlimactic, it's merely residuary.

On the one hand, in Keat's original English, his last question defines his position as struggling with how or whether to live in some existential nonexistent state. Wake? Sleep? Die? Live? Imagine? Experience? The last question defines Keats's past life up to that point in the poem and also his unknown, unknowable future. The last question punctuates the very nature of identity and also, most important, the very nature of lyric identity. Keats's question at the end of the "Nightingale" Ode is a defining moment, not just in this poem, but in the history of poetry in English, too. It says that the lyric self straddles the realms of the real and the imagined.

On the other hand, Roffi's reversal puts the emphasis at the end, not on the state of mind of the poet, but on the departing "music" of the bird. In the original, the image of the "music" is primarily concrete: it's the birdsong foremost with some average metaphoric resonance, I mean. But in Roffi's version, the "music" is now all-encompassing: it's the birdsong, it's the symbol for the imaginative life, it's a definition of the cycles of living and dying. It's like the fish that got away.

Roffi's English-to-Italian alteration may fix the poem with a more blunt and concretely thematic resolution. It may make the poem work better in Italian, I don't know. But it's a willful undoing of the original. And Roffi's translation makes me defensive for Keats and for a defining moment in English poetry, too—defensive in a way I don't usually feel when reading translations into English when my lack of familiarity with the other language softens into suspended disbelief.

And yet this state of translational affairs is as inevitable as it is troubling. You may be asking yourself how a reader can stay alert when confronting the peculiar elasticity of translation. Bilingual translations certainly help, as long as you are willing to take the time to compare the two languages and ponder the interaction between the author and the translator.

Regarding Roffi's "Ode to a Nightingale," I could say it would be worse for Italian literature not to have any Keats at all. And yet, some sacrifices just aren't worth defending.

To Slay Shakespeare

I sometimes ask beginning readers of poetry to name a poet whose work they like. One name that often tops the list is e. e. cummings.

Why cummings, I ask? The reply: Because cummings doesn't use punctuation or capitalization.

OK, I say, but you must like that his poems are a mixture of puzzle and wit, too?

Yes, they answer. He's totally original and fun.

And what about his poems' emotional swoon, I ask, their Indian summer variety of Romanticism? As in: "when by now and tree by leaf / she laughed his joy she cried his grief / bird by snow and stir by still / anyone's any was all to her." Or in these lines: "may i feel said he / (i'll squeal said she / just once said he) it's fun said she."

Yes, yes, they answer. Though now I often detect less conviction than their earlier assertions.

On the other hand, what bothers me about all this is the reasoning that e. e. cummings is so much fun because he's original and groundbreaking.

Fun, yes. Original and groundbreaking? Hardly.

As with any art, poems neither improve from one generation to the next nor are they ever entirely original. There's no graph to chart the improvement of poetry—like measuring the standard of living—though some may argue that the opposite is possible. Anyway, I put it to you that art doesn't improve. And poetry doesn't improve. But in every generation, there are always extraordinary poets whose poems define the times.

As a shape, poetry's historic development can be thought of as a spiral, and typically this spiral takes both a generational and patricidal-slash-matricidal spirit—and here I'm thinking in particular of the development of British and American poetry.

The generation of British poets who followed Shakespeare must have been flummoxed by his unparalleled virtuosity—I mean, how do you react against Shakespeare? Where do you go next as a writer to make something fresh after Shakespeare? How do you best the best of the Renaissance?

Eighteenth-century poets knew that Shakespeare was brilliant, yes, but he wasn't, well, perfect. So to slay Shakespeare, if you will, they sought inspiration from classical Greek poets and especially Roman poets from the Augustan era. That's how eighteenth-century poets became known as the New Augustans.

Nineteenth-century poets, deadened by New Augustan wit and coolness, which itself was a reaction against Renaissance fleshiness, re-adopted a warm, humanistic sensibility in order to slay their immediate forebears. Romantic poets infused an emotionalist spirit that was connected intimately with the natural world and the psyche.

Poets of the early twentieth century, stunned by the cruelties of the Great War and the threats from capitalist modernization, viewed nineteenth-century emotionalism as stagy. They saw those embellishments as unconvincingly soft and disconnected from the realities of their industrialized times.

Instead, these early twentieth-century poets sought to recapture the metaphysical intellectualism of the past—looking longingly at Elizabethan poets of the seventeenth century for inspiration. I should say: only some Americans looked there. Others wrapped themselves fully inside the morphological idioms of the American melting pot. And so in early twentieth-century poetry, wit once again became highly valued.

Are you asking, how does this relate to cummings's spirit of lust and high feeling?

I'll tell you. Another poet of that seventeenth-century period, who, like cummings, typified his age's interest in sartorial wit, was Michael Drayton.

Drayton (1563–1631) was a friend of Ben Jonson's and some think Shakespeare's, too. So when readers say, I love e. e. cummings, I say, you'll definitely love Michael Drayton because he was doing that e. e. cummings thing three hundred years earlier and cummings learned a lot from him. Here is Drayton's "Sonnet V":

Nothing but *No*, and *Aye*, and *Aye*, and *No?*
How falls it out so strangely you reply?
I tell ye, fair, I'll not be answered so,
With this affirming *No*, denying *Aye*.
I say "I love," you slightly answer *Aye;*
I say "you love," you pule me out a *No;*
I say "I die," you echo me an *Aye;*
"Save me," I cry, you sigh me out a *No;*
Must woe and I have nought but *No* and *Aye?*
No I am I, if I no more can have;
Answer no more, with silence make reply,
And let me take myself what I do crave.
    Let *No* and *Aye* with I and you be so;
    Then answer *No*, and *Aye*, and *Aye* and *No*.

I love these kinds of cross-century links in poetry, just as I love how a puzzling line by cummings—"when by now and tree by leaf"—echoes Drayton's teaser, "Must woe and I have nought but *No* and *Aye?*"

Literary connections across the generations affirm the traditions and influences under which poets of all ages must work. By embracing the idea that influences are real and nurturing and vital, readers can discover the depth and breadth of poetry's history, as well.

Struggle to the Finish

In the 1980s the American poet C. K. Williams published *Flesh and Blood*, a collection of 130 eight-line poems.

Is it something weirdly obsessive or wholly missionary that causes a poet or artist to work in one form repeatedly? Isn't the poet at risk, you might ask, of over-indulging in recurring narrative habits, turns of mind, and structural effects and therefore turning the project into a precious aesthetic study or, worse, a formulaic tick? Won't repeated use of a form limit a poet's ability for exploration and immersion?

One way to look at it is that a poet's immersion in one form is like a painter's extended work in a specific color palette or a single-sized canvas. The fixed number of lines, the limited colors, or the restricted canvas force the poet to see and imagine the world from within that single framework or filter and presumably to find pleasure—or at the very least to entertain a well-exercised interest—in repeatedly engaging the world through that form, as in C. K. Williams's poem "Repression":

> More and more lately, as, not even minding the slippages yet,
>   the aches and sad softenings,
> I settle into my other years, I notice how many of what I once
>   thought were evidences of repression,
> sexual or otherwise, now seem, in other people anyway,
>   to be varieties of dignity, withholding, tact,
> and sometimes even in myself, certain patiences I would have once
>   called lassitude, indifference,
> now seem possibly to be if not the rewards then at least
>   the unsuspected, undreamed-of conclusions

to many of the even-then-preposterous self-evolved disciplines,
   rigors, almost mortifications
I inflicted on myself in my starting-out days, improvement days,
   days when the idea alone of psychic peace,
of intellectual, of emotional quiet, the merest hint,
   would have meant inconceivable capitulation.

What could cause a poet to write over a hundred eight-line poems? It's a bit excessive, you think, no? And yet the immersion is a bulwark against "capitulation." Capitulations to what? I guess it's accepting the limitations of form and shape and the necessity to maximize the effects of language inside the structure of a poem. In other words, the limitation frees the imagination.

If poetry can sometimes be defined as the best words in the best order, as Samuel Coleridge said, then what better pressure for a poet than ordering those words within a fixed frame? And then testing that frame over and over.

Now, in the spirit of disclosure, I should say I wrote and published a book of forty-four nine-line poems, so I understand something of the impulse. Or compulsion. I understand something of the challenge that by working within a predetermined form (in Williams's case a rather short form of just eight lines), Williams would be able to eliminate almost all pressures for explication or gentle introduction. Beginning with the first line even, Williams immediately has to create drama. There's no time to warm up the poem's theme or subject or to ease into the poem's narrative.

In other words, he is playing with live ammo from the very first syllable of the poem.

This last point relates to something that's also central to writing lyric poetry—that poems don't build from a valley to a peak. I mean, a poem consists of a series of peaks with bottomless ravines in between.

Poetry, like any art, is high-risk. Failure is imminent. To write poems in a single form repeatedly is to risk artistic failure repeatedly. Because, strangely, after the ninth or tenth one you've completed, the form begins to push back against your efforts. And push back harder after the twentieth, the fiftieth, the hundredth one. It's as if the form develops its own laws and won't let you break them without exacting punishment. And the mandatory sentence is a failed poem.

This relationship between poet and poem, or poet and form, then, is a struggle to the finish—at the least it's a negotiation, since with the form fixed the poet must constantly change the content or subject (that is, the material) or be doomed to monotony.

How does a poet accomplish this? He does it by writing about a range of subjects: love, friendship, motherhood, work, illness, grief. Or by writing about one subject over and over again, hoping to capture its many various dimensions.

Renewed, Restored, and Brought Home

There's nothing more exciting than discovering a poet for the first time.

I remember reading T. S. Eliot's "The Love Song of J. Alfred Prufrock" when I was seventeen and shortly thereafter reading "The Waste Land," and thinking, this Eliot guy is hot!—not knowing that the rest of the Western world had deemed him hot fifty years earlier and that the Swedish Academy had chimed in too with a Nobel Prize in 1948.

At seventeen, what did I know? Yet even now, years later, just thinking about the excitement I felt reading Eliot for the first time, I can feel the waters of poetry parting again like a sea of possibility.

I remember reading the *Complete Poems* of John Keats the first time, too. It was during jury duty in Boston during the summer of 1986. His Odes left me with an idealized faith in the perfection of poetic language.

I remember the first time I read Seamus Heaney in the spring of 1989, when I was living in Washington, D.C. If you had seen me riding the Metro that year you would have seen my head, day after day, bent over his *Selected Poems*. Every one of his richly cadenced syllables made me feel as if I were breathing the linguistic and rhythmic air of human knowledge and poetic understanding.

What I'm speaking of, I guess, is the sensation of discovery.

When you find someone new or someone you've never read or read closely before, your entire perception of what poetry can do—even, what you never dreamed it could do—gets expanded. A fresh clarity

57

enters your consciousness. Most wonderful of all, your faith in poetic invocation is renewed, restored, and brought home—even if the most critically refined thing you can say is "wow" or (should you feel particularly urbane) "whoa," or you're left entirely speechless, just blowing a long high whistle of admiration.

Naturally, I can have extended periods when the thrill of discovery is remote. At times, it feels unattainable. But then something comes along that washes out the dullness.

That's how it was for me a few years back when I read the Danish poet Inger Christensen for the first time in a New Directions collection, *Butterfly Valley: A Requiem.* I started poking around the poems one afternoon, and two hours later my hair was on fire. "This Christensen lady is hot," I called out into the next room, and then just read these lines out loud to no one in particular:

> Up they soar, the planet's butterflies,
> pigments from the warm body of the earth,
> cinnabar, ochre, phosphor yellow, gold
> a swarm of basic elements aloft.
>
> Is this flickering of wings only a shoal
> of light particles, a quirk of perception?
> Is it the dreamed summer hour of my childhood
> shattered as by lightning lost in time?
>
> No, this is the angel of light, who can paint
> himself as dark mnemosyne Apollo,
> as copper, hawkmoth, swallowtail.
>
> I see them with my blurred understanding
> as feathers in the coverlet of haze
> in Brajcino Valley's noon-hot air.

Born in 1935 in Jutland and trained as an educator, Inger Christensen began publishing drama, essays, fiction, poetry, and children's books in the early 1960s. Her poems are elegant, formally inspired, and gutsy. She has a characteristic habit of devising knotty structures that express multifaceted ideas.

Butterfly Valley: A Requiem, from which the above selection comes, is a fifteen-part sonnet cycle on the theme of life arising from death. As if to dramatize her "blurred understanding" of life and death, Christensen reuses the last line of each sonnet as the first line of the next one. Then, at the end of the sequence, she recycles in her crown of sonnets all of the first lines of the previous fourteen to construct the fifteenth and final poem. A complex design to match a complex idea—one that details the limits of human understanding and confronts the transforming shock of mortality.

There's all that, true, but after I read Christensen for the first time I found myself experiencing that feeling of pure pleasure again. I was lost, I was found, I was speechless and in awe. Who knew she'd won the Swedish Academy's Nordic Prize? Who knew that Austria gave her its State Prize for Literature or that she's often cited as a Nobel contender and is one of Europe's most revered poets?

I was simply reading poetry, man. I was simply reading poetry.

Thingness

It was in Margaret Kennedy's second year Latin class at Bellaire High School in Houston—long before I'd begun thinking of writing poems myself—that I first read and translated the passion-drenched lyrics of the Roman poet Gaius Valerius Catullus.

Some say Latin is a dead language. But, really, each language remains alive, in Seamus Heaney's expression, with the music of what happens. A language remains vibrant both in the languages of the past and in the renditions of that language in the present.

Poets in particular experience a swell of reverie whenever the topic of the roots of words comes up. Want to see what I mean? Check out the etymology of the word "pratfall." If you're elated by what you find, there may be a poet lurking in you.

I'm certain that studying Latin influenced me to think of language not only as an etymological substance but also as a physical one. I began to see language as a transcultural medium that evolves across generations. Language is fertile and rich because of its chords, variations, and ambiguities. And now what I most cherish about words is their thingness.

If there is one person who first electrified my interest in both the fleshy simplicities and muscular complications of words, it was Mrs. Kennedy. If her Texas-sized hair was half the show, her "You cannot be serious!" rebukes to my fellow students' clumsy sight readings was the other half, except when her ire was directed at my translational stumbles, in which case I was plainly embarrassed. She taught with an ideal sort of professional dedication—not so much with regard for the very few students who took all four years of high school Latin with her as I did, but more for the Roman literati of her spirit life: Virgil,

Caesar, Apuleius, Cicero, Horace, Ovid, and especially Catullus, whose poems of desperate love, I think, she took personally, as in "Vivamus, Mea Lesbia":

> Let us live, my Lesbia, and love,
> And we'll figure a small coin
> To kill the rumors spread by old men.
> The sun sets and rises—for us,
> When our brief light sets,
> There remains unbroken night, and our sleep.
> Give me a thousand kisses, then a hundred kisses,
> Then another thousand, a second hundred.
> Then also another thousand! And again a hundred!
> Then, with many thousands—we've lost count,
> Confused, beyond all knowing!—
> Let not a rotten person be jealous of us
> Who knows of our endless kissing.

I'm not sure if it was Catullus's sensual depiction of longing or, if you can believe it, some contact high with the object of his affection—the married Clodia, whom Catullus immortalized as "Lesbia"—that I was more in the thrall of. Perhaps I was just in love with Clodia! If so, that love was akin to the way one falls in love with, say, Thomas Hardy's Tess or James Joyce's Michael Furey. It was a literary sort of love, a literary sort of lust.

I am sure that my translations for Mrs. Kennedy seldom surpassed the summarized versions of a Loeb Classical edition, and it crushes me to admit this.

Still and all, I have not forgotten the physical joy I felt, and still feel, from the whispered camaraderie of Catullus's poems. The first poem I had from memory was one of Catullus's self-inflicted stabs into the heart, "Odi Et Amo."

Surely you could chalk this interest up to adolescent infatuation on my part, or at least, to what was then my well-practiced concentration on unrequited love—"excrucior" is Catullus's word.

Catullus was born in Verona, in 84 BC, and became a friend of Julius Caesar's when Caesar was governor of Gaul. That's the Caesar of "Gallia est omnis divisa in partres tres," or "all Gaul is divided into three parts," for those of you now nostalgic for the Top-of-the-Pops mainstays of your first year Latin studies.

Living in Rome in his early twenties, Catullus met and fell in love with the married Clodia, ten years his senior, and had a brief affair with her until she dropped him for another lover. The consequence of being dumped led him to write love poem after love poem so that he was transforming his suffering into his art.

Not that he was inventing a literary feeling, mind you. After you've read the near-erotic cries in some of Catullus's poems and the pained woes of unrequited passion in others, it will not surprise you to learn Catullus adored the Greek poet Sappho, and translated some of her poems into Latin. Her influence on him is beyond simply noticeable.

"Vivamus, Mea Lesbia" is one of Catullus's sillier bedroom romps of a poem. As an invocation of sexual fantasy, it dramatizes sex not as romantic or tragic (that comes elsewhere), but as comic. And it provides you with a seriously good definition of poetry as the art of the sensual trance.

And that trance bridges the physical pleasure one gets from reading Catullus and other poets from the era of Caesar to late twentieth-century America.

From the Past to Here

Who would not sing for Lycidas?

"Your columns are OK and all," a Marion County woman wrote in one year. "But they don't help me understand anything about how poetry got from the past to here."

"Well, ma'am," I replied, "I can do that."

"Go ahead," Jeff Baker said when I brought the idea to him over lunch. "But you only get five thousand words for the entire history."

No surprise, but five thousand words proved impossible.

What follows in this section is a brief history of British and American poetry—with a lot of that history and a lot of that poetry obviously missing. Instead, what's here is the broad outline of the back-and-forth dialogue among poets across the generations from the Renaissance to the late twentieth century.

Look into Thy Heart and Write

Sir Philip Sidney (1554–1586), one of the most influential poets of the Renaissance, was just thirty-two years old when he died of a musket wound. Popular and revered—"Farewell, the worthiest knight that lived," Londoners cried out during his funeral procession—he was adored by queen and commoner.

His "Defense of Poetry" is the first critical statement on poetry in English. Not that it was wholly original—more like warmed-over Aristotle—but it's an excellent summary of Renaissance literary thought that envisioned poetry in English as a "speaking picture," believed that poetry revealed pleasure in pain, and affirmed intellectual inventiveness as literature's highest ideal.

The poet, for Sidney, was a second creator (God being the first) that creates a second nature (that is, creates art). And the purpose of art is to teach and delight. Poetry's responsibility is to lift readers into the perfection of the poem's universe.

The Philip Sidney bumper sticker for this aesthetic would read: "Look into thy heart and write."

His great sonnet series, "Astrophel and Stella," brings the star lover (Astrophel) in search of his unrequited star (Stella): "Come let me write. And to what end? To ease / A burdened heart."

In the "Sad Steps" sonnet, Astrophel flings his pain onto the object of the moon. His heart is broken, and therefore the whole world feels broken and sad, too:

> With how sad steps, O moon, thou climb'st the skies!
> How silently, and with how wan a face!
> What! may it be that even in heavenly place

That busy archer his sharp arrows tries?
Sure, if that long-with-love-acquainted eyes
Can judge of love, thou feel'st a lover's case:
I read it in thy looks; thy languished grace
To me, that feel the like, thy state descries.
Then, even of fellowship, O Moon, tell me,
Is constant love deemed there but want of wit?
Are beauties there as proud as here they be?
Do they above love to be loved, and yet
    Those lovers scorn whom that love doth possess?
    Do they call 'virtue' there—ungratefulness?

The Renaissance mind was not a post-Darwinian mind. Copernicus had established that the sun was the center of the solar system only a dozen years before Sidney was born. It was not unfathomable, at least in a literary sense, to wonder if there were some sort of aura of emotional consciousness up there on the moon's surface. That's why Astrophel asks the moon if there is "constant love" there, because on earth—as the bitter final four lines demonstrate—there surely is not.

But there's no answer from the moon, is there? That's typical of the Renaissance aesthetic, too. As with inconstant love, reality may be too painful to see. For Philip Sidney, a beautiful artifact like a poem is the ideal medium in which to extol that pain.

Full Belief

The Renaissance represents a period in which poets specialized in the emotions of the heart (say, in poems by Philip Sidney), the body (poems by William Shakespeare), and in the case of poet George Herbert (1593–1633), the spirit.

For Herbert, who wrote the famous dictum "his bark is worse than his bite," poetry is not merely a study of the physical pleasures of human existence. Instead, and of greater importance, poetry is the study of the metaphysical and spiritual pleasures of our time on earth.

Herbert's poetic interest focuses less on the everlasting heavenly dramas of Christian faith and more on the moments of being alive that possess eternal qualities. His strictly logical poems can often seem like subversive sermons—he was in fact, first and foremost, an Anglican deacon and later a priest.

Above all he is a figurative poet. Full belief in God is essentially his one subject. Meaning, he uses allegory and metaphorical argument to advance this emotion in his poems. He dramatizes the psychology of religious experience. He creates complex conceits, paradoxical images—all in a plainspoken, conversational tone. When you get to know his work, you can see how both the demeanor and the tone of his poems will later inspire Emily Dickinson, T. S. Eliot, and Wallace Stevens.

And yet even when Herbert feels alienated from God, as he sometimes does, his poems embody the ideal that reconciliation between the human and the divine must remain the believer's ultimate aim. So that in a poem such as "The Quip," God is both accessible and inaccessible, and sin and love are dramatized as mutual conduits to religious understanding:

The merry World did on a day
With his train-bands and mates agree
To meet together where I lay,
And all in sport to jeer at me.

First Beauty crept into a rose,
Which when I pluck'd not, "Sir," said she,
"Tell me, I pray, whose hands are those?"
But Thou shalt answer, Lord, for me.

Then Money came, and chinking still,
"What tune is this, poor man?" said he;
"I heard in music you had skill:"
But Thou shalt answer, Lord, for me.

Then came brave Glory puffing by
In silks that whistled, who but he?
He scarce allow'd me half an eye:
But Thou shalt answer, Lord, for me.

Then came quick Wit and Conversation,
And he would needs a comfort be,
And, to be short, make an oration:
But Thou shalt answer, Lord, for me.

Yet when the hour of Thy design
To answer these fine things shall come,
Speak not at large, say, I am Thine;
And then they have their answer home.

Whereas Herbert's contemporaries romanticize and idealize human love (like Sidney) or focus on the temporality of human love (like Shakespeare), Herbert writes that physical love leads to shame. That remorse, he argues, actually brings you closer to faith. How? Through confession and salvation.

In this sense, the source of both love and life, for Herbert, is individual conscience—where those eternal moments of being take shape. That's using poetry for radical intentions. Because through allegory and dialogue, a poem like "The Quip" insists that one's conscience ("I am Thine") is the source of spiritual clarity.

And if one's conscience can be represented in a single poem, how about one's relationship to the broader realms of religious faith, of religion, and in particular Protestant Christianity? It will take John Milton's epic imagination to write poetry of that scope.

In a Single Utterance

John Milton (1608–1674) called William Shakespeare "Fancy's child" and Robert Graves sweetly observed that "the remarkable thing about Shakespeare is that he really is very good, in spite of all the people who say he is very good."

Yes, Shakespeare certainly is very good.

But when you compare the poems with the plays, there's an argument to be made that they are not quite as good. So I'm going to sidestep Shakespeare's poems, and in particular the famous sonnets. Anyone wanting to understand even a little about the formulation of modern poetry would do well to look for essential sources and resources, not in Shakespeare's poems, but in his comedies and tragedies.

John Milton was no slouch either. He was the son of a scrivener, which makes him a kind of middle-class poet. He knew Galileo, and while active politically he was a bit of a liberal flunky. He worked for Cromwell and later was briefly jailed at the start of the Restoration of Charles II.

Milton took justifying the ways of God to man as his poetic calling. "Paradise Lost" is his prime achievement in English poetry. But it's also a fabulous anomaly in the generation-upon-generation conversation among poets. Being epic and not lyric, it has never felt particularly modern. The poem's moral argument can sometimes seem remote.

Milton's great elegy, "Lycidas," however, is a masterwork that still influences contemporary poets and is arguably the most important early elegy in English poetry. I'll go one more than that: "Lycidas" changed the nature of the lyric poem in English by bringing argument, doubt, lament, and celebration all together in a single utterance.

Published in 1638 when Milton was just twenty-nine, "Lycidas" elegizes Edward King, an acquaintance of Milton's from Cambridge, who had drowned in the Irish Sea. The poem confronts friendship, challenges ecclesiastical authority, attacks the pastoral, and links local experience with a variety of mythological impulses from Greek to Roman and from Anglo to Hebraic. All this in a mere 190-some lines. Here is the famous opening:

> Yet once more, O ye laurels, and once more
> Ye myrtles brown, with ivy never sere,
> I come to pluck your berries harsh and crude,
> And with forc'd fingers rude
> Shatter your leaves before the mellowing year.
> Bitter constraint and sad occasion dear
> Compels me to disturb your season due;
> For Lycidas is dead, dead ere his prime,
> Young Lycidas, and hath not left his peer.
> Who would not sing for Lycidas? he knew
> Himself to sing, and build the lofty rhyme.
> He must not float upon his wat'ry bier
> Unwept, and welter to the parching wind,
> Without the meed of some melodious tear.
>
> Begin then, Sisters of the sacred well
> That from beneath the seat of Jove doth spring;
> Begin, and somewhat loudly sweep the string.
> Hence with denial vain and coy excuse!
> So may some gentle muse
> With lucky words favour my destin'd urn,
> And as he passes turn
> And bid fair peace be to my sable shroud!

At the heart of the poem is the "uncouth swain." This idealized figure is Milton's characterization of the poet as an average person who aspires to attain universal truth.

We'll see this very conflict take shape in the next three poets featured in this series. First, American Colonial poet Anne Bradstreet will take up the mantle of the "uncouth swain" in writing about the truth of family life from a woman's perspective while also confronting a massive continent unexplored by Europeans in the seventeenth century.

During the chic London of the eighteenth century, Alexander Pope will attempt to pull poetry in the opposite direction from Milton, advocating for an idea of the poet as a master craftsman who attains truth through perfecting classical poetic forms.

Finally, in the nineteenth century, in the remote Lake District of England, William Wordsworth will realign English poetry once again with his beloved Milton ("Milton! thou shoulds't be living at this hour: / England hath need of thee"). He will dare poets to speak the "uncouth" truth about daily experience and to write about "incidents and situations from common life...in a selection of language really used by men."

Something for the Soul

Poetry in the American Colonial period was all ode-back-to-jolly-England obedience with little or none of the yawping American individualism we've come to know.

Head of the class in that era was a woman John Berryman would call "Mistress Bradstreet," a poet who wrote poems during a Puritan stasis in American life whose penal offenses included drunkenness, blasphemy, thespianism, and fornication.

Woo-hoo! Those were the days to be a wild artist!

Anne Bradstreet's Colonial era (she was born in 1612 and died in 1672) was one in which daily labor was considered a religious duty, moral rigor was favored over social gratification, and men and women were taught to distrust their natural, meaning sensual, inclinations. She was a devout Englishwoman when she set sail with her husband on the *Arabella* and settled in Salem, Massachusetts, in 1630. Both her father and her husband became governors of the Massachusetts Bay Colony. Her husband presided during the infamous witch trials.

Of her eight children, Bradstreet wrote: "I had eight birds hatched in one nest / Four cocks there were, and hens the rest." You can see from just these lines how unsubtle her style was, how knotted to English precedent of rhyme, meter, and caricature.

But don't take this to mean she was a simpleton. Because, like John Milton, Bradstreet writes from a belief that poetry ought to do something for the soul of its reader. But not at the expense of murdering the comedic—when you read "four cocks," you know what she means.

Her subjects are English history, biblical experience, Greek gods, and domestic life. This last category comprises the theme of her best work. Typical of the seventeenth-century criticism of her poems is the notion that she either was dabbling too much in a man's art or was simply mad.

None of that idiotic criticism mattered however.

Her work was wildly popular in England and in the New World. She became a "voice for the era," as one biographer put it. Today, she is remembered as both the first colonial settler and the first woman to publish a book of poems in England, *The Tenth Muse Lately Sprung Up in America*, in 1650.

With a mild fusion of secular and religious tension, her style most resembles Philip Sidney's, whom she read closely and admired. But: with their soft fog of a growing Americanness, Bradstreet's lyrics mark the beginning of a serious tension in poetry in the English-speaking world between British song and American speech—or the way "speech barks back at song," as Stanley Plumly puts it.

Stuck in the seventeenth century in the backwater of the colonies, Bradstreet was mostly whistling back toward home. A poem such as "To My Dear and Loving Husband" declares loving faith, allegiance, and union both with her husband and, by my reading, with England and English verse, too:

> If ever two were one, then surely we.
> If ever man were loved by wife, then thee.
> If ever wife was happy in a man,
> Compare with me, ye women, if you can.
> I prize thy love more than whole mines of gold,
> Or all the riches that the East doth hold.
> My love is such that rivers cannot quench,
> Nor ought but love from thee give recompense.
> Thy love is such I can no way repay;
> The heavens reward thee manifold, I pray.
> Then while we live, in love let's so persever,
> That when we live no more we may live ever.

You can draw a direct line from this concept of "reward" to the conflicts with reward in the work of a major twentieth-century American poet like Adrienne Rich. And you can see how far we've come from Colonial poetics. We've evolved from a poetry that sings of the rewards of obedience to a poetry that, quoting the title of a book by Rich (which itself quotes the ending phrase of *The Great Gatsby*), decries the dark fields of the Republic.

Rational Wit

When you turn your mind to the colicky and irascible Alexander Pope (1688–1744) and the new movement in English poetry he represents, you see the stark differences between the poetry of seventeenth-century Shakespeare and the eighteenth-century Enlightenment.

Alexander Pope was grumpy, petulant, and truculent. That was on his good days.

But he could write heroic couplets better than any poet of his era—and arguably any poet since. By focusing his wicked couplets on the foibles and hypocrisies of London society, he earned a ton of money doing it, too.

From generation to generation there is always an ongoing conversation among poets. But the conversation between the poets of the seventeenth and the eighteenth century, as I have said earlier in this book, almost stopped before it got going.

Where most generations revolt against the literary values, habits, styles, and successes of the previous one, how could you ever revolt against the greatest writer in all of English literature, William Shakespeare?

That challenge was the primary burden for poets of the eighteenth century.

So what did the English Enlightenment poets do? They tried to thread the needle. They believed that Shakespeare was brilliant, all right, but he wasn't perfect. His rhymes, his meters, his forms were all certainly OK, but they were not perfect.

So in form, style, and thought, perfection became the aim of poets like Alexander Pope.

Searching for the best models of formal perfection, Enlightenment poets looked beyond their forebears in the Renaissance to revered models from antiquity. They began to animate their poems with the certainties of the Augustan poets of the Roman era. Thus, the New Augustans were born. Alexander Pope was a leader of this reclamation of orderly scaffolding.

Where Renaissance poets, such as William Shakespeare, celebrate instinct, intuition, and spontaneity, the New Augustans thrive on skepticism, decorum, and refinement.

Where Renaissance poets value synthesis of experience with rhyme as a route to psychological discovery, Augustan poets favor rational wit and expressions of didactic authority—with rhyme as a means of intellectual control.

Where Renaissance poets love the sonnet, New Augustans favor the mock epic. "The imagination gilds all objects but alters none," writes Pope, believing that poetry is meant to give permanent expression to thought and experience.

There's all that, but let's not ignore that Alexander Pope could turn a memorable phrase. He is responsible for several widely repeated expressions in English over the last three centuries:

"To err is human; to forgive, divine."
"Know then thyself, presume not God to scan; / The proper study of mankind is man."
"Hope springs eternal in the human breast."
"A little learning is a dangerous thing."

Here is a terrific excerpt from Pope's poem, "Essay on Criticism":

> Such shameless bards we have; and yet 'tis true,
> There are as mad, abandon'd critics too.
> The bookful blockhead, ignorantly read,
> With loads of learned lumber in his head,
> With his own tongue still edifies his ears,
> And always list'ning to himself appears.
> All books he reads, and all he reads assails,
> From Dryden's Fables down to Durfey's Tales.
> With him, most authors steal their works, or buy;
> Garth did not write his own *Dispensary*.
> Name a new play, and he's the poet's friend,

Nay show'd his faults—but when would poets mend?
No place so sacred from such fops is barr'd,
Nor is Paul's church more safe than Paul's churchyard:
Nay, fly to altars; there they'll talk you dead:
For fools rush in where angels fear to tread.
Distrustful sense with modest caution speaks;
It still looks home, and short excursions makes;
But rattling nonsense in full volleys breaks;
And never shock'd, and never turn'd aside,
Bursts out, resistless, with a thund'ring tide.

Surely you recognize one of Pope's most famous lines. It comes about six lines from the bottom: "For fools rush in where angels fear to tread." It's a line that has been borrowed throughout the ages by an unlikely mixture of writers, politicians, and artists, most famously Edmund Burke, Abraham Lincoln, E. M. Forster, Frank Sinatra, Elvis Presley, and Bob Dylan. Only a few of whom would consider themselves children of the Augustans. And it is a line that thoroughly emboldens the post-Renaissance, neo-Augustan ideal of decorum and mastery over emotions.

The Literary and the Literal

William Wordsworth changes everything.

While poets from the sixteenth to the eighteenth centuries favored formality and decorum and emphasized the literary in their poetry, the bard of England's Lake District dazzles the nineteenth century with fresh language and an original vision about the relationship between the literary and the literal.

Today we consider Wordsworth a great nineteenth-century poet. But it's worth noting the date of his first book, *Lyrical Ballads*. It was published in 1798. Which is to say, Wordsworth is a nineteenth-century poet with an eighteenth-century education. He got involved in the French Revolution and then, frightened by its brutality, returned home with his enthusiasm for political and civic unrest considerably cooled.

In its place the pleasantness and mysteries and sometime dangers of Britain's natural environment became his primary interest.

You can see the natural world's influence on his new mind in three of his most famous dicta about poetry—beginning with writing that had organic virtues and an antipathy for "gaudy and inane phraseology." First, he believed that a poem should be a selection of "incidents and situations from common life." Second, a poem should be composed in a "language really spoken by men." Finally, "all good poetry is the spontaneous overflow of powerful feelings [and it] takes its origin from emotion recollected in tranquility."

You can get a sense of the difference in Wordsworth's own writing between the literary and the literal in this quatrain:

> Calm is all nature as a resting wheel.
> The kine are couched upon the dewy grass;

> The horse alone, seen dimly as I pass,
> Is cropping audibly his later meal

The first two lines, to me at least, seem literary. Nature is compared to a wheel. The cows are poeticized as "kine" and "couched" in a belletristic figuration of "dewy grass." But the second two lines seem plainly literal: the horse is barely visible and simply eating.

As in these lines from "Composed upon Westminster Bridge, September 3, 1802," Wordsworth's best writing would come to exemplify the second two lines. His poems would become an exhibition of spontaneity with a nimble feel for common life:

> Earth has not anything to show more fair:
> Dull would he be of soul who could pass by
> A sight so touching in its majesty:
> This City now doth, like a garment, wear
> The beauty of the morning; silent, bare,
> Ships, towers, domes, theatres, and temples lie
> Open unto the fields, and to the sky;
> All bright and glittering in the smokeless air.
> Never did sun more beautifully steep
> In his first splendour, valley, rock, or hill;
> Ne'er saw I, never felt, a calm so deep!
> The river glideth at his own sweet will:
> Dear God! the very houses seem asleep;
> And all that mighty heart is lying still!

Wordsworth emphasizes a correspondence between nature and the inner life where the self and the imagination are supreme. This, alone, is his greatest argument against Pope's poetry of social authority. And it's Wordsworth's greatest legacy.

For Wordsworth, poetry is simply not an argument—as it was for Pope and Herbert and Bradstreet. Instead, poetry is a mood, an emotion, and a way of feeling that distills experience.

That's why Wordsworth's poems changed everything. His definition of poetry's sensory importance has come to dominate the thinking and the making of poetry in English for the past two centuries.

So: William Wordsworth changes everything. Until John Keats changes everything again.

The Subject of Poetry

From the time he began publishing poems in his early twenties through his tragic death at the age of twenty-five, and then beyond into his posthumous afterlife as a Romantic poet *sui generis*, John Keats's literary reputation weaved from reviled to respected to unknown.

Today, he is renowned. He's an enshrined poet of unparalleled lyric achievement in English. F. Scott Fitzgerald once extolled the experience of reading Keats by saying, "For a while after you quit Keats all other poetry seems to be only whistling or humming."

If Wordsworth's poems opened the door to a poetics of feeling—that a poem is "emotion recollected in tranquility"—then Keats's poems are the Romantic pinnacle of Wordsworthian values.

John Keats was born in 1795. His father kept a livery stable and died in 1804, thrown from a horse. Keats's mother died of consumption when the boy was a teenager. A brother, Tom, would also die of consumption when Keats was in his early twenties. John nursed him—caught it—and that led to his death in an apartment at the foot of the Spanish Steps in Rome in 1821.

With little money and few real prospects, Keats lived a pauper's life and suffered a prolonged, painful death. But his poems represent a golden poetic ideal—namely, that the subject of poetry is poetry itself. Even at his best, Keats is a horribly self-conscious poet who believed that poetry could release you from the stream of time through a delirium of the senses and that vividness and sensuality are the route to authentic emotion.

Poetry, he wrote in a letter, must "surprise by a fine excess." If you know Milton, you can see why Keats adored the epic poet for his exquisite sense of both passion and pleasure.

Where nature for Wordsworth is the primary source for poetic material, its uses (as poetic material) for Keats are limited to nature's explicit connection to art. Keats believed that a poem must strive for the infinite. He was certain that there exists both a real world of mortality and also an ideal world of permanence.

Poetry, he argued, makes life permanent.

In the end, Keats believed that a poet is a chameleon. A poet is "the most unpoetical thing in existence," he wrote, an idea that gets full presentation in "On First Looking into Chapman's Homer":

> Much have I travell'd in the realms of gold,
> And many goodly states and kingdoms seen;
> Round many western islands have I been
> Which bards in fealty to Apollo hold.
> Oft of one wide expanse had I been told
> That deep-browed Homer ruled as his demesne;
> Yet did I never breathe its pure serene
> Till I heard Chapman speak out loud and bold:
> Then felt I like some watcher of the skies
> When a new planet swims into his ken;
> Or like stout Cortez when with eagle eyes
> He star'd at the Pacific—and all his men
> Look'd at each other with a wild surmise
> Silent, upon a peak in Darien.

Because a poet has no "Identity—he is continually" receding into the work of art he creates. This Keatsian idea is the Romantic legacy we carry today, seen so clearly in a sonnet like "On First Looking into Chapman's Homer." Here is a poem that elevates intuition over reason and turns the poet into his poem.

Individuality and Equality

If John Keats believed that a poet is the "least poetical thing in existence," then it might be said that Walt Whitman believed a poet is the most democratic thing in existence. The post-Revolution and pre-Civil War America, Whitman contended, needed to develop a "great original literature." But not only that, Whitman had a special, even religious faith that this new American literature would "become the justification and reliance, (in some respects the sole reliance,) of American democracy." The poet "is a seer . . . he is individual . . . he is complete in himself . . . the others are as good as he, only he sees it and they do not."

In other words, *e pluribus poetus*: out of many, the poet.

And if only one poet can truly be called the most American of American poets, there's a good case to be made that it should be Walt Whitman. Born in 1819 on Long Island, Whitman grew up in Brooklyn, lived in Washington, D.C., during the Civil War, and died in Camden, New Jersey, in 1892, at the age of seventy-two. As a young man Whitman floundered as a partisan journalist and printer in New York and at night tried to write traditional poetry. Lacking the patience and discipline needed to control rhyme and meter, these early efforts were mostly failures.

During the 1850s, though, Whitman broke his style when he began to rearrange his prose journals into long lines of biblically cadenced free verse. During the summer of 1855, he self-published his masterpiece, *Leaves of Grass*. The first edition was ninety-five pages long, with a dozen untitled experiments. He would devote the rest of his life to revising and expanding the book, and by 1881, *Leaves of Grass* contained 293 poems on 382 pages.

The book's great achievement is the poem "Song of Myself," which begins "I celebrate myself, and sing myself, / And what I assume you shall assume, / For every atom belonging to me as good belongs to you."

Just that beginning line, "I celebrate myself, and sing myself" was startling, shocking, and new.

Of its six words, half are first person pronouns and the other two are words of exhilaration—celebrate and sing. And, I have to ask: To sing myself—what does that mean? In one sense, it foreshadows Abraham Lincoln's conclusion in the Gettysburg Address, for Whitman sings of myself, by myself, and for myself. Or is myself an object, as in "to sing Bach?" To sing myself.

By opening his imagination and his poetic forms, Whitman's project involved more than just defining himself. He wanted to be, as a poet, the poetic representative of the American people. For sure this was a controversial ambition, because Whitman was homosexual. So, along with his writings, he was publicly condemned in 1881 by the Society for the Suppression of Vice. Even Emily Dickinson refused to read him, saying she had heard his poetry was "disgraceful."

The following selection, from the 1881 version, comes almost exactly in the middle of "Song of Myself." The early editions had been published without Whitman's name on the jacket. It's here that he identifies himself as the author of what will become one of the most important books of poetry in human history:

> Walt Whitman, a kosmos, of Manhattan the son,
> Turbulent, fleshy, sensual, eating, drinking and breeding,
> No sentimentalist, no stander above men and women
>   or apart from them,
> No more modest than immodest.
>
> Unscrew the locks from the doors!
> Unscrew the doors themselves from their jambs!
>
> Whoever degrades another degrades me,
> And whatever is done or said returns at last to me.
>
> Through me the afflatus surging and surging, through me
>   the current and index.

I speak the pass-word primeval, I give the sign of democracy,
By God! I will accept nothing which all cannot have
     their counterpart of on the same terms.

Through me many long dumb voices,
Voices of the interminable generations of prisoners and slaves,
Voices of the diseas'd and despairing and of thieves and dwarfs,
Voices of cycles of preparation and accretion,
And of the threads that connect the stars, and of wombs
     and of the father-stuff,
And of the rights of them the others are down upon,
Of the deform'd, trivial, flat, foolish, despised,
Fog in the air, beetles rolling balls of dung.

Through me forbidden voices,
Voices of sexes and lusts, voices veil'd and I remove the veil,
Voices indecent by me clarified and transfigur'd.

This is an example of a poet clarifying his passion for individuality and for a desire to be the poetic voice ("through me") for individuality. And he makes the democratic American claim that he's an individual among a collective, that he is among the many "threads that can connect the stars."

Can poetry be the art form to honor such high ambition? That's best left unknown. But this much is known: even when we use a framework such as individuality and equality to discuss poetry, poetry works on readers differently. A poem infiltrates a democratic dialogue one reader at a time. It's like the ballot in the voting box. You read it and cast your vote privately. In so doing, you assume what all Americans assume, that you are the embodiment of *e pluribus unum*.

Closed for the Season

"If we have time, let's stop at Emily Dickinson's house," I suggest to my college-touring son as we wheel into Amherst, Massachusetts, on a rainy day during Lent. Sure, he says, tossing in a belated jibe, "Maybe it'll be open this time."

Funny, sad, and yet too true. He was well-acquainted with my sorry track record as a visitor to the Dickinson homestead at 280 Main Street.

This would become my seventh attempt—and seventh failed attempt—to actually enter the brick house that has stood near the Amherst town square since 1813 when Dickinson's grandparents built it. I'm not kidding! This time: "Closed for the season." We were two weeks too early.

So I would not get a chance, yet again, to go inside the house and see the desk Emily Dickinson used to write her nearly two thousand poems, nor prowl around her demure parlor, nor, from upstairs, stare into the spring garden as she would have. I would not see that blank canvas of a courtyard that so inspired her vision and that was the surging impulse for her fierce imagination.

Instead, I'd have to be content—again—with standing in the driveway, disappointed, and loitering around the fence and hemlock hedges.

I've met a lot of people who try to read Emily Dickinson's fabulous poems and have a similar relationship with her poems as I do with her house. They just can't get inside. To these readers, Dickinson's poems come across as cryptic, interior, and, you know, closed.

I want to say to those of you who have struggled this way, please persist. There's a lot to enjoy by lurking around in the Dickinson driveway, a lot to behold from examining the outer-scapes as a means to live fully in the inner-scapes.

To begin with, Emily Dickinson is that rare poet who can look outward and inward at the same time, as when she writes:

> As imperceptibly as Grief
> The Summer lapsed away—

Consider this: where Walt Whitman aims outward as a means to embrace the fullness of lived experience at a macro and cosmic level, Emily Dickinson steers inward. Then, going inward into fancy, mind, and spirit, she reveals a spectacular segment of the cosmos of her subconscious.

By that, I mean she is a poet who encloses.

More like John Keats than William Wordsworth, more like Philip Sidney than George Herbert, Dickinson brings private insight to both the life of the mind and the life of the body. So when she writes in "As imperceptibly as Grief" that "The Dusk drew earlier in—/ The morning foreign shone—" it's ambiguous whether she means you to read those characterizations as being about the weather or about her spirit:

> As imperceptibly as Grief
> The Summer lapsed away—
> Too imperceptible at last
> To seem like Perfidy—
> A Quietness distilled
> As Twilight long begun,
> Or Nature spending with herself
> Sequestered Afternoon—
> The Dusk drew earlier in—
> The morning foreign shone—
> A courteous, yet harrowing Grace,
> As Guest, that would be gone—
> And thus, without a Wing,
> Or service of a Keel
> Our Summer made her light escape
> Into the Beautiful—

From outside the Dickinson house—sadly the very place in Amherst, Massachusetts, that I know best—as you look around at the adjoining neighborhood and the heart of the town and the windows up to her secluded rooms, you can get a feeling from those lines that, surely, she means both inner and outer. That's the thing about her poems: they are interested in ambiguities of volition in terms of how we perceive and what we perceive.

And isn't that aesthetic about perception one of the most enduring and riveting legacies of Emily Dickinson in American poetry?

The Armory Show

The intergenerational conversation among poets teeter-totters across centuries between, on the one hand, a poet's interest in the linguistic medium of the art and, on the other hand, the poet's interest in the experiences of a lived life.

Two twentieth-century American poets epitomize this dichotomy: Wallace Stevens and Elizabeth Bishop. One is a poet of the expressionistic variety, the other a poet in the representational mode.

American poet Wallace Stevens (1879–1955) had all but given up ambitions to write poetry as a young man in the early 1910s, settling instead into the beginning of what would be a lifelong legal career working in the insurance industry. But after he attended the landmark Armory Show of 1913, Stevens was more than inspired to take up the writing of new poems and, even while working a corporate day job, to forge new parameters of the American poetic experience.

The Armory Show is a signature event in the history of American art. The show was America's introduction to Modernism. The artists in the show rejected landscape, representational, and holistic art in favor of interior, abstract, and fractured art. The exhibition included over a thousand paintings and sculptures by some three hundred avant-garde artists, including George Bellows, Pierre Bonnard, Mary Cassatt, Paul Cezanne, Camille Corot, Marcel Duchamp, Paul Gauguin, Vincent Van Gogh, Wassily Kandinsky, Edouard Manet, Henri Matisse, Claude Monet, Pablo Picasso, Camille Pissarro, Joseph Stella, and many others.

The experience left Stevens undone.

Returning to his writing, he filled his notebooks and early poems with gorgeous language, exotic images, expressionistic landscapes, sumptuous music, vivid inventions of consciousness, and abstract meditations. What Stevens brings to the dialogue among poets is a poetics that attests to the inner inventions both of the self and of the mind's perceptions. Stevens's poems are not devoid of experience, but assert the mind as central to poetry's existence. Should one's imagination die, he argues in his great poem, "The Plain Sense of Things," one's physical life would cease to exist, too.

"The imagination loses vitality as it ceases to adhere to what is real," Stevens once wrote. The imagination, he says, "adheres to the unreal and intensifies what is unreal, while its first effect may be extraordinary, that effect is the maximum effect that it will ever have."

You get a good sense of Stevens's ideas about the real and the unreal in his collage-style poem "Study of Two Pears," which blends the imagery of a common fruit with the abstract vision of a painting:

I

Opusculum paedagogum.
The pears are not viols,
Nudes or bottles.
They resemble nothing else.

II

They are yellow forms
Composed of curves
Bulging toward the base.
They are touched red.

III

They are not flat surfaces
Having curved outlines.
They are round
Tapering toward the top.

IV

In the way they are modeled
There are bits of blue.
A hard dry leaf hangs
From the stem.

V

The yellow glistens.
It glistens with various yellows,
Citrons, oranges and greens
Flowering over the skin.

VI

The shadows of the pears
Are blobs on the green cloth.
The pears are not seen
As the observer wills.

Here is a poetic parallel to Duchamp's "Nude Descending a Staircase."
The pear is less food and more a conceived aesthetic form. It is less
about nature and meant, instead, as an occasion to inspire artifice.
Less a poem composed from experience and more one composed from
invention.

This inventiveness would be Stevens's influence on American po-
etry, an influence about a negotiation both toward and against rational
linguistic playfulness, innovative interior territories, and grand medi-
tative lyricism.

Discretion

Beginning with Philip Sidney and George Herbert, moving through John Milton and Anne Bradstreet and Alexander Pope, then to William Wordsworth and John Keats and Walt Whitman and Emily Dickinson and Wallace Stevens, there is a progression of poets talking back and forth across the centuries about the meaning and role of the imagination and of poetry.

We've seen Philip Sidney's poems suffused with the heart's desires, George Herbert's poems about the physical pleasures of faith, Alexander Pope's poems about society's foibles, William Wordsworth's poems about the emotional centers of experience, John Keats's poems about the perfection of art, Walt Whitman's poems of democratic vistas, and Emily Dickinson's fierce domestic mind. We've seen Wallace Stevens writing about the supreme fictions of the imagination. And now, Elizabeth Bishop writing about the sturdy facts of human existence.

One side for art, the other for life.

One side for the dominance of language, the other for the dominance of experience.

One side for inventing a mask to vivify human experience, the other for responding directly to humanity.

These dichotomies detail the give and take British and American poets have engaged in for hundreds of years and across multiple generations. When you determine which concentration is in force in a given poem, you're more easily able to understand the poet's values.

American poet Elizabeth Bishop (1911–1979) falls on the side of responding directly to lived experience. She has become one of the most widely praised poets of our era for the way in which she chronicles the fusion of self with culture. David Orr could not contain his praise for her in 2008 when he wrote in the *Times*: "You are living in a world created by Elizabeth Bishop. Granted, our culture owes its shape to plenty of other forces—Hollywood, Microsoft, Rachael Ray—but nothing matches the impact of a great artist, and in the second half of the twentieth century, no American artist in any medium was greater than Bishop. That she worked in one of our country's least popular fields, poetry, doesn't matter. That she was a woman doesn't matter. That she was gay doesn't matter. That she was an alcoholic, an expatriate and essentially an orphan—none of this matters. What matters is that she left behind a body of work that teaches us, as Italo Calvino once said of literature generally, 'a method subtle and flexible enough to be the same thing as an absence of any method whatever.'"

Where Wallace Stevens's method is to be inventive, Bishop's is to be attentive, as in the opening of her poem "At the Fishhouses":

> Although it is a cold evening,
> down by one of the fishhouses
> an old man sits netting,
> his net, in the gloaming almost invisible,
> a dark purple-brown,
> and his shuttle worn and polished.
> The air smells so strong of codfish
> it makes one's nose run and one's eyes water.
> The five fishhouses have steeply peaked roofs
> and narrow, cleated gangplanks slant up
> to storerooms in the gables
> for the wheelbarrows to be pushed up and down on.
> All is silver: the heavy surface of the sea,
> swelling slowly as if considering spilling over,
> is opaque, but the silver of the benches,
> the lobster pots, and masts, scattered
> among the wild jagged rocks,
> is of an apparent translucence
> like the small old buildings with an emerald moss
> growing on their shoreward walls.
> The big fish tubs are completely lined
> with layers of beautiful herring scales
> and the wheelbarrows are similarly plastered

with creamy iridescent coats of mail,
with small iridescent flies crawling on them.
Up on the little slope behind the houses,
set in the sparse bright sprinkle of grass,
is an ancient wooden capstan,
cracked, with two long bleached handles
and some melancholy stains, like dried blood,
where the ironwork has rusted.
The old man accepts a Lucky Strike.
He was a friend of my grandfather.
We talk of the decline in the population
and of codfish and herring
while he waits for a herring boat to come in.
There are sequins on his vest and on his thumb.
He has scraped the scales, the principal beauty,
from unnumbered fish with that black old knife,
the blade of which is almost worn away.

She never once affects a rhetorical flourish, never affects a voice that is anything but conversational, never confesses the chatter of her life nor exploits it nor glorifies it. Instead, she writes with distilled and shy discretion. She observes. She eyes. She gathers. She tallies.

Bishop is a poet of manners, restraint, and subtlety—so unlike Alexander Pope's crassness or Walt Whitman's bombast or even, at times, Emily Dickinson's retorts. In "At the Fishhouses" you see this coolness in the closing lines of the poem:

I have seen it over and over, the same sea, the same,
slightly, indifferently swinging above the stones,
icily free above the stones,
above the stones and then the world.
If you should dip your hand in,
your wrist would ache immediately,
your bones would begin to ache and your hand would burn
as if the water were a transmutation of fire
that feeds on stones and burns with a dark gray flame.
If you tasted it, it would first taste bitter,
then briny, then surely burn your tongue.
It is like what we imagine knowledge to be:

dark, salt, clear, moving, utterly free,
drawn from the cold hard mouth
of the world, derived from the rocky breasts
forever, flowing and drawn, and since
our knowledge is historical, flowing, and flown.

These lines reveal a poet who holds back—holds back herself, the forces of nature, and the burdens of time. In this sense, she is more like George Herbert striving for poise in the face of spiritual chaos, or William Wordsworth offering insights into the "spots of time / Which with distinct pre-eminence" enliven and define our consciousnesses.

Bishop immerses her art into fact. She trusts in knowledge and conveys lived experience with the sharpness, clarity, and fine filigree-made imagery of a poet in the thrall of what exists right in front of her eyes. Observation of a real world, whether that world is tactile or of the subconscious, has become one of the dominant concentrations of a lot of American poetry ever since.

Obviously the story of poetry's ongoing conversation doesn't come to an end with the death, in 1979, of Elizabeth Bishop. Unfortunately this brief history of their conversation will end here.

Bishop's influence loomed large in American poetry, perhaps peaking at the turn of the twenty-first century as poets grew weary of the cohesive authenticity in both form and mind that her poetry represents. In reaction, many new poets have come to favor disruptive and nonlinear styles of thinking and writing. Just as in the past, the new generation rebels against the beliefs and values of its forebears.

In time, whether from artistic anxiety or distrust, aesthetic, historical, or political realignments, skepticism or frustration, demurral, outright rejection or just plain boredom, a future generation will turn its back on this current one. And the conversation will continue with new poems and a new—well, to be fair to the past, to honor the past, to claim the best of the past, and to reanimate and refresh the past—a renewed poetics will emerge.

Theories of Thumb

A different element, almost . . .

The Imperfectly Known

Richard Wilbur defines metaphor as the business to which all poetry is aimed: "It seems to me there has to be a sudden, confident sense that there is an exploitable and interesting relationship between something perceived out there and something in the way of incipient meaning within you. And what you see out there has to be seen freshly."

I love this definition. It's tethered to two crucial factors in writing a poem: aesthetic discipline and artistic chance.

Thinking about it now, I can see how metaphor, even as an essential characteristic of an enduring poem, remains one of the most complicated, even mysterious, tools for a poet.

Why does a poet use metaphor?

For one thing, metaphor helps attain clarity, but not clarity completely and not a scientific sort of clarity. The goal for metaphor is transformation. For example, consider the following simile: "The girl runs like a gazelle." I'm comparing the speed of the girl to the even greater speed of a gazelle, yes, but I'm not completely transforming this fast girl into something else. I'm not altering your perspective on speed. What I mean is, the "girl" and the "gazelle" remain compared but also separate and distinct.

On the other hand, when I write "The girl is a gazelle," I'm fusing girl and gazelle into one thing, eliminating their separateness, transfiguring the girl into a gazelle, making her a new creature. Metaphor requires this combination of interpretation, illustration, and vivification in order to make a fresh and unique comparison.

Consider this famous metaphor from the nineteenth century. Walt Whitman answers the question "what is the grass?" by saying "it must be the flag of my disposition" and also "it is the handkerchief of the Lord" and also "a uniform hieroglyphic, / And it means, Sprouting alike in broad zones and narrow zones, / Growing among black folks as among white, / Kanuck, Tuckahoe, Congressman, Cuff . . ." and also he says it is "the beautiful uncut hair of graves." He is using metaphor to clarify the unknown, or at least to clarify what is imperfectly known. He is revivifying what he knows, and what we know, about the meaning of grass, and the grass itself.

Yannis Ritsos (1909–1990), one of Greece's most important and beloved poets, accomplishes something of this in his startling poem "Women." The poem, translated here by Kimon Friar, is both about suffering and about the anxiety of imminent grief:

Women are very distant. Their bedsheets smell of good-night.
They leave bread on the table so we won't feel they've gone.
Then we understand we were to blame. We get up from the chair
    and say:
"You've overtired yourself today," or "Don't bother, I'll light the
    lamp myself."

When we strike a match, she turns slowly and goes
toward the kitchen with an inexplicable concentration. Her back
is a sad, small mountain laden with many dead—
the family dead, her dead, and your own death.
You hear the old floorboards creaking under her footsteps,
you hear the dishes weeping in the dishracks, and then that train
is heard taking soldiers to the front.

The local metaphors here—*smell of good-night, dishes weeping*—particularize a feeling of comfort under strain. The extended metaphor in the center of the poem—"Her back / is a sad, small mountain laden with many dead— / the family dead, her dead, and your own death"—presents the woman not just as a woman, but as a composite for the ways that women historically suffer the debilitation of wartime. She represents the domestic, yes, but in a larger context she becomes the state itself, awaiting news about the fate of the nation. And, as a figure, she is characteristic of metaphor's yardage, the distance it can travel to fuse perceptions.

I see this poem as something that relates to Wilbur's proposition, that metaphor represents "an exploitable and interesting relationship" between ideas. That's what a poem is, too, really. It's a metaphor from start to finish. The whole thing is a metaphor, a comparison in language, lines, and stanzas, in which the literary draws from actual experience and becomes a new experience.

Continuous Music

It happens more often than I care to admit. Some smarty says in the course of a conversation that he can't stand poems that rhyme, and when he happens onto a poem that rhymes—as if he just trips over them everywhere he goes—he says he's easily bored and can't read on.

Or not bored, but as a matter of principle won't read it. I'm not making this up. People have said this to me.

The worst offenders are aspiring poets.

It's hard for me not to take it personally, too, and I want to respond: C'mon, are we going to write off centuries of poetry in our very own language? Should we start with Shakespeare? Donne? Hardy? Dickinson? Is it goodbye, Geoffrey Chaucer? Goodbye, Alexander Pope? Is it possible today that so many English-speaking poets cannot fathom any fresh means to combine rhyme with contemporary idiom?

To be sure, writing poems with rhyme or writing poems without rhyme is never, and I mean never, the issue for a poem or for a poet. Rhyming provides a means to think. It utilizes the raw sounds of language as an expression of the sophisticated aspects of one's mind. It's a way to unify sound and sense, whether that unison is inspired, melodic, contrapuntal, or scandalous.

Consider one of W. H. Auden's rhymes: *ephemeral/beautiful*. Its musical echo is nearly pure. Its meaning as a word-pair—that beauty is short-lived—is also true.

All that I've said above characterizes rhyme in a technical way. But I like to think of a lyric poem in and of itself as the ultimate rhyme—the entire poem, I mean, not just its interior, ornamental, and echoing effects. From beginning to end, a poem is a sound, a voice, a continuous music that approximates and echoes its subject.

Imagine listening to poetry in a language you don't speak. You can delight in hearing the recurring parallel sounds. You can understand the feeling and the musical essence of the meaning—the mood and the gist of the poem become apparent to you. That's the spirit of rhyme.

I've always liked the way Christian Wiman uses regular and ir-regular rhyming patterns in his work. Wiman was born in West Texas in 1966, attended Washington & Lee University and Stanford University as a Stegner Fellow, and served as editor of *Poetry* magazine for ten years.

Original and evocative, his poems recall, in the best sense, the poetry of Seamus Heaney for the texture of the music, and the poetry of Philip Larkin for the poignant doubt.

"Rhymes for a Watertower" is typical Wiman rhyming:

> A town so flat a grave's a hill,
>   A dusk the color of beer.
> A row of schooldesks shadows fill,
>   A row of houses near.
>
> A courthouse spreading to its lawn,
>   A bank clock's lingering heat.
> A gleam of storefronts not quite gone,
>   A courthouse in the street.
>
> A different element, almost,
>   A dry creek brimming black.
> A light to lure the darkness close,
>   A light to keep it back.

The pair of rhymes *lawn/gone* intimates the mood of the poem. But the rhyme pairing that gets me when I read "Rhymes for a Water-tower" is the closing one in the final stanza. This one, *skin/again*:

> A time so still a heart's a sound,
>   A moon the color of skin.
> A pumpjack bowing to the ground,
>   Again, again, again.

What this rhyme says is identical to how it says it. That's the combined intellectual and emotional effect rhyme is after. In this way rhyme affirms the experience of recognition both as a rhyme (*skin/again*) and within its buried repetitions ("again, again, again").

Rhymes such as these are like a second skin for the poem's argument and meaning. From the beginning of the poem until the concluding word, I hear a beautiful, rhythmic interpretation and awareness of experience. I hear the music of rhyme carrying the heartbeat of the literary ("sound") into the existence of experience ("ground") in a way that shows poetry's core relationship to how we might understand our lives.

Spiral of the Imagination

As a sequence of lines, a poem stretches both over the latitudes of a page with horizontal intensity and cruises down the page with vertical drive. I've come to imagine this shape—across and down, repeatedly—to be like a spiral of the imagination.

Then, imposed on this spiral are a poem's sentences.

You could call the interplay between lines and syntax the lyric grammar of a poem for the way it frames a poem's moments of experience and formulates its emotional rhythm. Yielding and cohering, this grammar discloses what is isolated, subordinated, and coordinated among the images, tones, voice, melodies, and narratives of a poem.

Talvikki Ansel's "World," for example, is a single stanza with twenty-nine lines composed of thirteen sentences:

> Olive green of pond water, tea-
> colored is the newt's body.
> Legs stroking, it floats close
> to the surface, lazily circles
> the dock's posts, a fish
> swallowing in the shallows.
> Its feet once walked moss, logs—
> a world and name, *eft*, left behind.
> Pin-points of vermilion
> freckle its skin. It nudges
> under floating leaves blown down
> from the trees. Saturdays,
> the zebra-striped plane flies up

from the neighboring fields.
Its roar follows the tree edge,
our pork-chop-shaped parcel of land,
turns back at the boundary. Over
the woods, over the dock,
narrow trails and deer paths,
the dead tree where the vulture roosts.
A finite number of times the engine
will go up, up. The zebra in the circus
ring prances round. Rises
the snapping turtle's triangle face
from the mud. My wishing to nudge
the days larger, longer. A girl's run
in the woods at dusk—blue shorts
the hunters saw briefly as the deer's
flickering of blue sky.

Six of the sentences finish at the very end of a line, while seven finish in the middle of a line. Nearly half of the sentences are about two lines long, while the longest is four lines long. None of these numerical facts tell you a thing about the meaning or intent of her poem, with its keenly observed Virginia landscape. But the arrangement of lines and sentences can tell you about the composition of the moments, the accruing worlds, inside the poem.

Now look back at the poem again.

The first sentence comprises two lines, is adjective-heavy (*olive green, pond, tea-colored, newt's*), and sets out the degrees by which the patterns of the natural world are invoked.

By the time you get down to the series of short sentences (one per line practically) near the end of the poem, you might get the feeling that the poem is desperate to increase the "finite number" of things to be observed. It's here that the poet is "wishing to nudge" even more things into the poem, to locate all that is "flickering" in the world.

Ansel's sense of the physicality of lines and sentences represents one of poetry's distinctive elements, to relocate and reorganize the textures of consciousness and daily life into a grammar and lineation of ideas and emotions.

Born in 1962 to a boat-maker father and a librarian mother, Talvikki Ansel grew up in Connecticut, was educated at Mount

Holyoke College, the University of Indiana, and Stanford. Her poems echo the intense lyricism of European poets like Fernando Pessoa of Portugal and the Italian Eugenio Montale. In the spirit of disclosure, I first read her poems when we were Stegner Fellows together at Stanford University in the mid-1990s. Poets in that workshop were already in command of their art. There were some fine poets in our group, too, including Kevin Young, Christian Wiman, and Emily Warn. Ansel's singular originality stood out. As in "World," her poems even then were rich with a microscopic lyricism ("a world and name, *eft*, left behind").

Ansel's first book, *My Shining Archipelago*, was the Yale Series of Younger Poets selection for 1997. The series editor at the time, James Dickey, praised her poems for the way in which they "render the heat, the closeness, the mystery, and the terrible fear of the undisclosed, the lurking, the waiting to happen."

That's just the feeling I get in the poem's last sentence when, at the end of a line and in the midst of a syntactic fragment, a girl suddenly enters the landscape and, just as suddenly, hunters you don't even know are there are startled by her appearance.

Distinct Routes

Poets arrive at the making of a poem from two distinct routes. One route is to begin with an experience through memory and then to shift toward discovering the language that will render and transform the memory into a poem.

The other route is to begin with the medium of language itself and then to locate in the imagination experiences that the language evokes and invokes.

Either way, the pathways will eventually feed one another.

For instance, you have an experience of riding an unruly horse and you decide you need to write a poem. The experience speaks for itself: you did ride the horse, and it did buck you off. You write:

> Hercules was fat and roan-dark as a cloud
> And ran me off the trail
> All that summer day in the mountains.

But just recording experience is not enough. A piece of writing that just reports what happened is not a poem. It's an executive summary.

So you investigate the language of the experience—some good places to start are with the horse's name, its color, and the metaphors inside the weather. You conjure horse words (*hoof, mane, gee, haw, gallop*), Hercules-myth words (*labors, Augean stable*), and cloudy-weather words (*rain, thunder, sleet*).

Then by steering your imagination into the language of the experience, you discover meanings to transform the experience into a poem. Now you have something new:

> Hercules was fat and roan-dark as a cloud
> and thundered me all that rain-trailed day
> into the labors of the summer mountains.

In the other method, or through the other sensibility, the poet begins far from remembered experience. For instance, you're interested in writing about hues and shades of light. You think: I will write about the color brown because I want to know what brown means. You think of the forms, shapes, and existences of brown-ness. You imagine brown objects, you imagine brown animals. Then, for no logical reason, you remember the brown horse from that rough trail ride—and there you are, locating experience from the language. You write: "Hercules was fat and roan-dark as a cloud…"

In Emily Warn's poem, "The House of Musing," she starts not just with language but with the Hebrew alphabet:

> The trick? To live without survival kits:
> miracles, bottled water, fire starters, spells.
>
> To stop grumbling to God and build
> your hut in the wilderness.
>
> No need to search or not search.
> Just join hay stalk to hay stalk, bale to bale
>
> until thick walls swathed with mud appear.
> From within, the doorway frames the quiet
>
> of a tree with a single leaf. You're safe
> to examine the distance you've crossed.
>
> How you lived not knowing you lived.
> How you postponed this reckoning
>
> believing you lacked a desire to know.
> Yet here you are listening to a leaf
>
> scrape air, your hands smeared with mud.

Warn has described how the Hebrew alphabet became her obsession, how it gave her the tools and the filter to find experience. "The complex meanings that have accrued to the [Hebrew] letters themselves," she has said, "all relate in some way to their three attributes—their shapes, names, and numbers—and to where and how the letters and the words they constitute appear in the Torah. Similar to some Chinese characters, the shapes of many Hebrew letters resemble forms found in the world.... For example, *beit*, the second letter ... is shaped like a house ... and its name means 'house.'"

"The House of Musing" is a poem of self-instruction. It came about from Warn's musing about *beit*, the second letter of the Hebrew alphabet. It came about by first beginning with language as a medium—like color, like wood, like marble—and finding the narratives embedded there. Whether a poet begins with memory or begins with the medium of language doesn't really matter in the end. Because during the process of writing a poem, she will find herself shifting back and forth between the urgencies of both. The imagination's routes and roots are deep and interconnected. One of the enduring pleasures of writing and reading poetry is to remain open to the confluences that the art of language offers to the individual poet and that the individual poet returns to the art.

Ceremonial Rite

In addition to being engaged and entertained by a poem's ideas, techniques, expression, form, and subject matter, a lot of people will tell you that they want to feel something after reading a poem. And they want to feel that the poet has felt something, too.

"No tears in the writer, no tears in the reader" is how Robert Frost puts it.

Sometimes it's not easy to distill what a poem's emotion is—and often there's more than one emotion cooking anyway. Which is to say, the relationship between emotional states in a poem can be ambiguous. Because we value ambiguity in poetry, that's nothing to be bothered by really. To read poetry is to seek pleasure in the convergence of multiple emotions and multiple meanings.

A poem's emotion can accumulate gradually or emerge with a sudden shock. It can be unclear even until the very end, as in Rainer Maria Rilke's influential sonnet "Archaic Torso of Apollo," in which for thirteen-and-a-half lines he observes a statue in exquisite detail only to conclude with an emotional burst of courage and rapture in the last five words of the poem, "You must change your life."

Michael Collier's "Confessional" has just this sort of emotional ambiguity:

> I was waiting for the frequency of my attention
> to be turned to an inner station—all my mind but trivial matter,
> wavelengths modulated like topiary swans on a topiary sea,
> and not quite knowing where the tide would take me.
>
> In the darkness where I kneeled, I heard whispering,
> like dry leaves. It had a smell—beeswax, smoke;

a color—black; and a shape like a thumb.
That's when the door slid open and the light that years ago

spoke to me, spoke again, and through the veil,
an arm, like a hand-headed snake, worked through,
seven-fingered, each tipped with sin. What the snake couldn't see,
I saw, even as it felt what I felt or heard what I said.

Then along my arms boils and welts rose, on my back
scourge marks burned. I counted nails, thorns.
In my mind, inside my own death's head, I could hear: "Please,
forgive me. Do not punish me for what I cannot be."

The mixture of feelings here includes apprehension, composure, fa-
miliarity, unconscious gratitude, a hint of terror, unhappiness and,
given the title of the poem, repentance.

Collier's "Confessional" acknowledges a hard-wired pressure to
make an admission about the desire for—but the inability to attain—
faith. It professes a sort of non-faith even when asking for forgiveness
and mercy. You might conclude that the exact words that stir the
poem's emotion include *topiary, darkness, whispering, spoke to me, veil,
rose, forgive, punish*. Taken together, these words characterize Collier's
difficult disclosure. They dramatize the complex emotion that is
intrinsic both to the psychological condition and to the ceremonial
rite of confession.

Michael Collier's elegant poems have always contained a spiritual
richness. The author of many books of poetry, editor of several an-
thologies, and translator of the Greek tragedy "Medea," he was born
in 1953 in Phoenix where he was educated first by nuns at the Institute
of the Blessed Virgin Mary and then in high school by Jesuits, before
studying with William Meredith at Connecticut College.

Thinking of the influence of his early Catholic education, he once
said, "The idea that you came to an understanding of your purpose
in life by listening to a voice that was both inside and outside of you
was appealing to me because it was so mysterious." The emotion in
"Confessional" seems overwhelmed by that mystery, too, as it unveils
what can and cannot exist in a single human life.

More than that: it exhibits one of poetry's most crucial character-
istics. A poem discriminates among its emotions. It catalogues the

ambiguities. It finds pleasure in an inexact exactness, what we often simply call one's synthesis of thoughts and feelings.

Reverberation

One of lyric poetry's ambitions is to tender the nuances of our contemporary language into its most heightened fashion in order to answer the enormous, emotional question: What does it mean to be human?

Using the language of the present, the now, the that-which-we-say-now and see-with-now, a poet examines both what we have been—in the past, in history, in memory—and what lies in the future of life, death, and eternity.

One pleasure in reading poems that have this ambition is experiencing multiple shades of language. It can be enjoyable to notice how words in a poem ricochet between intention and meaning, meaning and surprise, and surprise and delight in the lightest and deepest etymological, even phonological ways.

There's a passage in an early poem called "Digging" by the Irish poet Seamus Heaney that is situated in this fashion. Heaney has just described a memory of ancestors digging potatoes and is letting that memory entice him: "The cold smell of potato mould, the squelch and slap / Of soggy peat, the curt cuts of an edge / Through living roots awaken in my head." The roots being dug up are the roots of the potatoes. That's the intention in the language and in the observation.

But the roots he's also digging for are the roots anchored in time that absorb the past, that are underground in consciousness, and that are embedded in perceptions expressed neatly in the exact language of digging up roots (*squelch, slap, curt cuts*). Heaney's root digging is a metaphor for the process of imagination and memory. The layered meaning of the phrase "living roots" delights me, at least, with its naturalness and its rightness.

You can see this sort of linguistic reverberation in Natasha

Trethewey's poem "Pilgrimage." The poem opens with an engraved sense of experience:

> Here, the Mississippi carved
>   its mud-dark path, a graveyard
>
> for skeletons of sunken riverboats.
>   Here, the river changed its course,
>
> turning away from the city
>   as one turns, forgetting, from the past—
>
> the abandoned bluffs, land sloping up
>   above the river's bend—where now
>
> the Yazoo fills the Mississippi's empty bed.
>   Here, the dead stand up in stone, white
>
> marble, on Confederate Avenue.

There are various inscriptions being carved here. There's the river and the riverboats. There's a contemporary city and the remaking of a past. There's the reapplication of history—the Confederate States of America are made ornamental in both name and recognition as a single street.

The poem then turns to acknowledge how those particulars echo with the poet's reality:

> I stand
>   on ground once hollowed by a web of caves;
>
> they must have seemed like catacombs,
>   in 1863, to the woman sitting in her parlor,
>
> candlelit, underground. I can see her
>   listening to shells explode, writing herself
>
> into history, asking *what is to become*
>   *of all the living things in this place?*

This whole city is a grave. Every spring—
    Pilgrimage—the living come to mingle

with the dead, brush against their cold shoulders
    in the long hallways, listen all night

to their silence and indifference, relive
    their dying on the green battlefield.

Now the engraving has become more ghostly and "hollowed by a web." Now the poet wonders what is the consequence of this ingrained history, what is reverberating among the elements of intention, meaning, surprise, and delight.

    Here you see how a museum exhibition, like a poem in some ways, investigates the consequences of experience. So when "Pilgrimage" turns to the brick and mortar depository of memory, both the ghost of experience and the ghost of memory share the same body:

At the museum, we marvel at their clothes—
    preserved under glass—so much smaller

than our own, as if those who wore them
    were only children. We sleep in their beds,

the old mansions hunkered on the bluffs, draped
    in flowers—funereal—a blur

of petals against the river's gray.
    The brochure in my room calls this

living history. The brass plate on the door reads
    Prissy's Room. A window frames

the river's crawl toward the Gulf. In my dream,
    the ghost of history lies down beside me,

rolls over, pins me beneath a heavy arm.

Sometimes it's just worth noting a bit of poetic delight, like the pun embedded in "hollowed" (think: hallowed) as well as the death words and battle words in the poem such as "underground" and "hunkered." The poem's last image, too, of a lifeless soldier ("pins me beneath a heavy arm") especially echoes the battlefield terror of the Civil War experience Trethewey is examining, on the one hand, and exposes, on the other hand, her awareness of being pinned by private and intimate anxieties.

These reverberations give poetry something more than just an effect of artifice. They make poetry exist as "living history," too.

Trethewey was born in Gulfport, Mississippi, in 1966. She often comes at her core subject—the immediacy and roots of American racial experience—by focusing both on her parents' interracial marriage in the segregated South and on the legacy of Southern slavery as a wicked mixture of lingering violence, pathos, guilt, and—strangely—kitsch. To mix these divergent elements requires a poet's careful touch and sense of arrangement, plus a studied attention toward the resonant resemblances and undertones of words.

Dreamy, Enigmatic, Generous, and Seductive

"Speaking for myself," W. H. Auden said in his 1956 inaugural lecture as Professor of Poetry at Oxford University, "the questions which interest me most when reading a poem are two. The first is technical: 'Here is a verbal contraption. How does it work?' The second is, in the broadest sense, moral. 'What kind of guy inhabits this poem? What is his notion of the good life or the good place? His notion of the Evil One? What does he conceal from the reader? What does he conceal even from himself?'"

Auden's questions have deeply influenced my reading habits. His first question concerns the inner mechanisms of a poem, the letter and spirit of its generous and seductive strategies as a made object, the slip-stitch of its formal seams, its very livingness.

Certainly the same framework holds with prose poems. Prose poems have, in a literary sense, nineteenth-century French genealogy and use many of the means of poetic composition available to a poet, except the ones that typically define a poem on the page, lines and stanzas.

To make up for the elimination of lines and stanzas, prose poems are often extremely self-consciously poetic and tend to be a paragraph or a few paragraphs in length. That prose poems are poetry at all is debatable, but not questionable. Today, prose poems are near the center of American poetry's contemporary zeitgeist, especially among younger poets.

I've always loved reading the Swedish poet Tomas Tranströmer's prose poems. "Answers to Letters" is one of my favorites. It is dreamy, enigmatic, generous and seductive:

In the bottom drawer of my desk I found a letter that first arrived twenty-six years ago. A letter in panic, and it's still breathing when it arrives the second time.

A house has five windows: through four of them the day shines clear and still. The fifth faces a black sky, thunder and storm. I stand at the fifth window. The letter.

Sometimes an abyss opens between Tuesday and Wednesday but twenty-six years could pass in a moment. Time is not a straight line, it's more of a labyrinth, and if you press close to the wall at the right place you can hear the hurrying steps and the voices, you can hear yourself walking past on the other side.

Was the letter ever answered? I don't remember, it *was* long ago. The countless thresholds of the sea kept migrating. The heart kept leaping from second to second like a toad in the wet grass of an August night.

The unanswered letters pile up, like cirrostratus clouds promising bad weather. They make the sunbeams lusterless. One day I will answer. One day when I am dead and can at last concentrate. Or at least so far away from here that I can find myself again. When I'm walking, newly arrived, in the big city, on 125th Street, in the wind on the street of dancing garbage. I who love to stay off and vanish in the crowd, a capital T in the endless mass of the text.

Notice all of the poetic devices in play in this passage of prose. There is a series of juxtapositions. There is reliance on a governing metaphor ("abyss") and the metaphor is developed into a conceit about the unanswered letter. There is the use of assonance, consonance, and parallel structures (in this translation by Robin Fulton, at least). And there is a handful of figurative devices from symbol to personification to irony.

Tranströmer, who was born in Stockholm in 1931 and who has been translated into more than fifty languages, has a wonderful manner and style and an ability to shift from one seemingly unconnected observation or experience to another in a way that makes you feel that the observations and experiences have always been somehow intimately connected.

As for Auden's second question, what kind of moral imagination inhabits this poem? Tranströmer defines his announced subject—a letter—with dreamy, enigmatic life, and history, and emotional crises: "A letter in panic, and it's still breathing when it arrives the second time." His description confirms a capacity for empathy and retrieval.

When Tranströmer squares up against the "labyrinth" of time and the "voices" of eternity, he refuses to rationalize his own failures—not answering the letter, or not remembering if he answered it. The subject of the poem is not communication, but time. Time is depicted as an experience and a happening where the "countless thresholds of the sea kept migrating."

This is a clear vision of a good life and a good place, as well as a notion of the Evil One. It all adds up to a poem that ripples with moral sincerity.

Finally, the poet transforms himself into a letter, the letter that begins his own name—T—to become the needed and desirable object that makes up words and metaphors. The poet becomes a shape, a sign, a scratch, a meaning, a dream, and an enigma, mutating from man to means and from means to art. By becoming just one of thousands, one of millions, a thing in time, a timeless thing, Tranströmer dramatizes the seductiveness of the poetic act.

Bottomless Mud

Since satire in poetry is both a type of poem and a tone, a satirist's methods of invective are diverse.

Whether working through mockery, sarcasm, or understatement, whether condemning vice or outing pomposity, a satiric poet's interests have less to do with lyricism or transcendence, and more to do with social, public, and moral commentary. Or outrage.

Few themes give a satiric poet so obvious a target as war. Most war poems, not surprisingly, are expressions of pacifism—though there are exceptions, such as Walt Whitman's pre-Civil War buffoonery, "Blow, Bugles, Blow." (To be fair, after a time, Whitman would come full circle on the war with his conscientious masterpiece, his elegy for Abraham Lincoln, "When Lilacs Last in the Dooryard Bloom'd.")

Siegfried Sassoon's upside-down sonnet, "Memorial Tablet," shreds post-Edwardian England's flag-waving strut into the Great War, especially the bizarre practice of wealthy households demanding that one of their servants volunteer for service in place of the master or the master's son's:

> Squire nagged and bullied till I went to fight,
> (Under Lord Derby's Scheme). I died in hell—
> (They called it Passchendaele). My wound was slight,
> And I was hobbling back; and then a shell
> Burst slick upon the duck-boards: so I fell
> Into the bottomless mud, and lost the light.
>
> At sermon-time, while Squire is in his pew,
> He gives my gilded name a thoughtful stare:
> For, though low down upon the list, I'm there;

'In proud and glorious memory' . . . that's my due.
Two bleeding years I fought in France, for Squire:
I suffered anguish that he's never guessed.
Once I came home on leave: and then went west . . .
What greater glory could a man desire?

This is a poem that defies the easy narratives of war, both at the front and at home, as simply being a difference between "glorious" and "bleeding." Because there was a real urgency for upper society households in World War I England to be seen doing their part for the war effort, their solution was both brilliant and ghastly. They made a showing of making a patriotic "sacrifice" by forcing one of the house's lowly footmen to volunteer for the front. This irony finds a place in Sassoon's poem as it ends with the question, "What greater glory could a man desire?"

Sassoon was born in 1886 in Kent and volunteered for the British military just prior to August 1914, when England declared war on Germany. His allegiance was stirred by the day's jingoistic propaganda. Once in uniform, he was admired—in an expression much in vogue in the day—as a gentleman warrior.

Sassoon was ruthless in battle but after his brother was killed in the disaster at Gallipoli and Sassoon descended into the moral murkiness of World War I's trenches, his enthusiasm waned. His patriotism plunged into sullen, confused depression. With the war winding down, Sassoon tossed his Military Cross into the river and refused orders to return to the front. The refusal didn't stick. When he did return to battle, he was injured in the head by friendly fire.

By the time he died in 1967, Sassoon had published nearly three dozen books of poetry and prose. Along with Robert Graves, Wilfred Owen, Rupert Brooke, and other British poets of the World War I generation, Sassoon mourned not just the futile brutality of chemical and trench warfare, but also the decimation of an entire generation of European men. Over eight hundred thousand British soldiers were killed in the four-year war. This is significantly fewer than soldiers killed from France (1.3 million), Russia (1.8 million), and Germany (2 million).

Even today, those numbers and what they signify—the gruesome toll on proud families and civil society—is obscene. The war ended, the Treaty of Versailles was inked, and the much-praised peace was, in the end, just a pointless prelude to something worse, World War II.

This, you could say, is the "bottomless mud" that Sassoon mocks, endless war brought on by pompous and incompetent leaders, for whom poetry does well to give one particular sort of salute: satiric condemnation.

A Good Ear and a Sharp Tongue

When I think about humorous poems—what we call light verse—I often wonder why it is that light verse has such a low critical reputation. It can't be that we're more grateful for poems of dying, despair, and unrequited love—though we do value poetry's magnificent habit of celebrating the fullness of emptiness.

Whether witty, ingenious, mordant, cynical, satirical, epigrammatic, whimsical, nonsensical, ironic, cool, neat, savage, ribald, or punning, light verse requires that its poet be a master of a playful conversational tone while at the same time demonstrating formal polish and elegance. In other words, the poet must have a good ear and a sharp tongue.

To enjoy light verse is to be willing to accept enchantment, such as:
Christina Rossetti's gleefulness:

> Mother shake the cherry-tree,
>   Susan catch a cherry;
> Oh how funny that will be,
>   Let's be merry!

Edgar Allan Poe's felicity:

> Keeping time, time, time,
> In a sort of Runic rhyme,
> To the tintinnabulation that so musically swells
> From the bells, bells, bells, bells
> Bells, bells, bells—
> From the jingling and the tinkling of the bells.

Vachel Lindsay's mirth:

> The Grasshopper, the grasshopper,
> I will explain to you:—
> He is the Brownies' racehorse,
> The Fairies' Kangaroo.

Langston Hughes's charm:

> Little snail,
> Dreaming you go.
> Weather and rose
> Is all you know.
>
> Weather and rose
> Is all you see,
> Drinking
> The dewdrop's
> Mystery.

Emily Dickinson's delectation:

> A bird came down the Walk—
> He did not know I saw—
> He bit an Angleworm in halves
> And ate the fellow, raw,
>
> And then he drank a Dew
> From a convenient Grass—
> And then hopped sidewise to the Wall
> To let a Beetle pass—

And Dickinson again, this time in a spirit of rapture:

> I never saw a Moor.
> I never saw the Sea—
> Yet know I how the Heather looks
> And what a Billow be—

I never spoke with God,
Nor visited in Heaven—
Yet certain am I of the spot
As if the Checks were given—

The Victorians tellingly referred to light verse as *vers de société*. One of its curators, the British critic Frederick Locker-Lampson, defines it as poetry where "sentiment never surges into passion, and where humour never overflows into boisterous merriment." Samuel Coleridge put it this way, insisting that light poetry is the "blossom and the fragrancy of all human knowledge, human thoughts, human passions, emotions, and language."

Wendy Cope's villanelle "Reading Scheme" has all this, plus a contemporary edge crystallized by parodying early childhood readers. Cope, who is on record for hating the term light verse, was born in Kent in 1945. Her work might remind you of the American humorist Dorothy Parker, whose casual touch, like Cope's, can be wicked, as in Parker's four-line poem, "Experience," that goes, "Some men break your heart in two,/ Some men fawn and flatter,/ Some men never look at you;/ And that cleans up the matter."

Here is a complementary quatrain by Cope, also about love between the sexes: "Bloody men are like bloody buses—/ You wait for about a year/ And as soon as one approaches your stop/ Two or three others appear."

Sometimes Wendy Cope just can't help the silliness of it, such as in "Making Cocoa for Kingsley Amis," another four-line ditty: "It was a dream I had last week/ And some kind of record seemed vital. / I knew it wouldn't be much of a poem/ But I love the title." In its fashion, Cope's giddy "Reading Scheme" accepts the burden for pleasure, too:

Here is Peter. Here is Jane. They like fun.
Jane has a big doll. Peter has a ball.
Look, Jane, look! Look at the dog! See him run!

Here is Mummy. She has baked a bun.
Here is the milkman. He has come to call.
Here is Peter. Here is Jane. They like fun.

Go Peter! Go Jane! Come, milkman, come!
The milkman likes Mummy. She likes them all.
Look, Jane, look! Look at the dog! See him run!

Here are the curtains. They shut out the sun.
Let us peep! On tiptoe Jane! You are small!
Here is Peter. Here is Jane. They like fun.

I hear a car, Jane. The milkman looks glum.
Here is Daddy in his car. Daddy is tall.
Look, Jane, look! Look at the dog! See him run!

Daddy looks very cross. Has he a gun?
Up milkman! Up milkman! Over the wall!
Here is Peter. Here is Jane. They like fun.
Look, Jane, look! Look at the dog! See him run!

Light verse jokes to tell the truth, and in this way it's not patently different from other poetry, determined, as all poetry is, to report and apprehend, to be both a flash and a revelation.

Revolt Against Logic

The Peruvian poet Cesar Vallejo was born in Santiago de Chuco in 1892, the last of eleven children. Disdainful of the orthodoxy of his Catholic youth, he became a Marxist and anti-Fascist, and actively supported the revolution in Spain.

One irony of his death in March 1938—he'd been living in Paris, poorer than a beggar and bouncing around with his wife in fleabag hotels—is that it occurred not only on Good Friday but also the day Franco's army marched into Madrid.

His poetry was widely read and imitated in this country in the 1960s and 1970s, thanks to translations by Robert Bly, James Wright, and others. These Midwestern poets internalized Vallejo's vigorous style into their poems, and brought a South American rather than a French brand of surrealism into North American poetry. There was a faddish quality to this new embrace of surrealism. In its defense, it opened American poetry to a fresh resource and a renewed appreciation for the distortive and the extravagant.

For a poet, surrealism offers liberation from received literary habits and conventions. Images are all-important and often placed in extreme juxtapositions. Language is fashioned to be elevated and absurd. Meaning is conveyed as ambiguous, ironic, mysterious, and psychological. With its associative, convulsive, swirling explorations of dreams, hallucinations, and the subconscious, the surrealist poem revolts against the limitations of logic and parades against reason.

"Under the Poplars" comes from Vallejo's influential 1919 book *The Black Heralds*, translated here by Rebecca Seiferle:

Like priestly imprisoned poets,
the poplars of blood have fallen asleep.
On the hills, the flocks of Bethlehem
chew arias of grass at sunset.

You see the mixture of sense and images right away with the "poplars of blood" and the "arias of grass." This surreal concoction goes on:

The ancient shepherd, who shivers
at the last martyrdoms of light,
in his Easter eyes has caught
a purebred flock of stars.

Formed in orphanhood, he goes down
with rumors of burial to the praying field,
and the sheep bells are seasoned with shadow.

Here we experience extreme conditions of reality. Stars roam in a herd. Bells have not just sounds but shadows. The disorienting universe is stacked against survival until, finally, the feeling gets resolved:

It survives, the blue warped
In iron, and on it, pupils shrouded,
A dog etches its pastoral howl.

Sometimes blasphemous, other times merely irreverent, Vallejo's surrealistic imagery, tone, diction, and themes confront colonialism, pastoral traditions, and religious conformity. "Under the Poplars" glistens with explosive, religious metaphor: "poplars of blood," "flocks of Bethlehem," "arias of grass," "martyrdoms of light," "Easter eyes," "seasoned with shadow," "pastoral howl." The juxtapositions inflame the differences between spiritual and naturalistic impulses.

For instance, "pastoral howl" combines the simple and idyllic "pastoral" with the violent and despairing "howl." A poem like "Under the Poplars" isn't built on a preconceived understanding of craftsmanship, artistic decorum, or reality. Instead, it's ripped from the chaos of experience with a brute gesture of super- or hyper-reality.

Poetry like his can release you from narrow expectations of the censoring, rational parts of your psyche. André Breton calls this release a locating of the "hidden places" of the psyche, where contra-dictions—past and future, real and imaginary—are wiped out. What remains is a perilous and thrilling contortion of reality and imagina-tion.

Camaraderie and Humility

When the Polish poet and Nobel Laureate Czeslaw Milosz died in Krakow in August 2004, a friend was traveling in Poland at the time and emailed the news to me. "Even the cabbies are weeping," he said, then ended "in Krakow, all the instruments agree, it's a dark, cold day."

If the phrases in that last expression seem familiar to you, it's because my friend was paying respect to Milosz by paraphrasing W. H. Auden's great elegy for William Butler Yeats, in particular the lines, "O all the instruments agree / the day of his death was a dark, cold day."

One beautiful tradition among poets is writing an elegy for a fellow poet. Auden's elegy for Yeats is—for me, at least—one of the best of the twentieth century. Here's a passage: "Earth, receive an honoured guest: / William Yeats is laid to rest. / Let the Irish vessel lie / Emptied of its poetry." This quatrain captures the sense of a serious loss, it remembers Yeats the man, and it pays homage to his poetry by echoing Yeats's style.

Two linchpins of this tradition of poets writing elegies for fellow poets are Shelley's 1821 poem for John Keats, "Adonais" ("The soul of Adonais, like a star, / Beacons from the abode where the Eternal are") and Milton's 1637 masterwork, "Lycidas." Elegies ceremonialize the advent of grief, the emotional burden of grief, and the necessity to reclaim life.

Traditionally the elegy was conditioned on a specific verse form with a particular metrical pattern. Surprisingly, it was not especially concerned with mortality. Over time the elegy has come to mean a poem that offers both lament and solace on the occasion of death.

An elegy for a fellow poet adds one more thing. It contains some expression—in form and in spirit—of admiration and homage for the art of the deceased poet. "Stern," the Irish poet Seamus Heaney's elegy for his friend, the British poet Ted Hughes, adopts the awkward, urgent angularity of a Hughes poem:

> "And what was it like," I ask him,
> "Meeting Eliot?"
> "When he looked at you,"
> He said, "it was like standing on a quay
> Watching the prow of the *Queen Mary*
> Come towards you, very slowly."
> Now it seems
> I'm standing on a pierhead watching him
> All the while watching me as he rows out
> And a wooden end-stopped stern
> Labours and shimmers and dips,
> Making no real headway.

What you have here is an elegy with multiple allegiances. "Stern" begins by alluding to another major poet, T. S. Eliot, whom a younger Ted Hughes compares to a looming ocean liner. Heaney concludes with a humanized nautical image of Hughes as a solid and stalwart rower. When you get right down to it, an elegy from poet to poet is partly for the benefit of the deceased poet and partly for the loss to poetry, too. It's a family thing.

I should mention another aspect of the poet's elegy for a fellow poet. It epitomizes camaraderie and humility. When W. S. Merwin concludes his elegy for a whole host of poets, "Lament for the Makers," by saying "the clear note they were hearing / never promised anything / but the true sound of brevity / that will go on after me," he's addressing the notion that though a poet's body and flesh must die, the body of work endures. In writing elegies for each other, poets honor the fundamental nature of poetry as a made thing that is a shimmering of language composed by someone who lived among us.

Wordless Ache

When Noel Arnaud wrote, "I am the space where I am," he was talking about the way the continuum of our past experiences and emotional selves continuously intersect with our daily lives. Or, as William Faulkner once put it, referring to the past in a broader context: "The past is not dead. In fact, it's not even past."

With titles of books like *In the Outer Dark, Out-of-the-Body Travel,* and *Now That My Father Lies Down Beside Me,* Stanley Plumly has written poems since the 1960s that oscillate between the chambers of absence and presence, memory and experience, and time and place. His poem "Silent Heart Attack" begins:

> When silence is another kind of violence.
> Like all the breath you've ever breathed
> suddenly swallowed. But since it happened
> over days, each night a little worse,
> it lacked the drama of my father's death.
> He went down, like a building, on his knees.

This opening assessment about silence as "another kind of violence" is a provocative claim, to be sure, and one that raises some questions. What is the nature of silence exactly? What is our language for silence? Is silence benign or malignant, or both?

For Plumly, who was born in Ohio in 1939, the luminous moments of a poet's personal history gestate in the imagination. Here is the poem's conclusion:

> I sat in the dark inside the feeling
> I was turning into stone, or, if I turned

around, to salt, salt crystals diamonding
the blackouts. Silence is what you hear,
the mouth a moon of Os, black filling up
the body with its blood. I listened.
Each night, all night, my father louder.

When you think about this poem's narrative frame, you can see how this poem dramatizes the silent heart attacks experienced by the poet. If that were all it were, we might not have a poem. But by emphasizing the language of the heart—as it exists both in normalcy and in crises (with words like *breath* and *swallow*)—the poem reveals how nearly impossible it is, figuratively speaking, to hear the differences. When Plumly alludes to his father's death, he neatly defines the psychological space between the past and the present. That is a place where the poet can sit "in the dark inside the feeling."

This last phrase is worth reading closely. It describes a place in the imagination where both memory and consciousness exist—the gestation zone. They exist in "the dark inside" the self. This entire line suggests that the elements of synchronicity between past and present fuse inside one's "feeling." And, also, the line suggests that understanding one's continuum of being-ness means to be aware of the nuances of that "feeling." In other words, poetry exemplifies the ideal that "I am the space where I am." And "I am the space where I am" is where a poem begins.

But a poem also begins in language: "Language is a darkness pulled out of us," Plumly once wrote as if to suggest that we always carry the language of our pasts, like secluded coves of solitude, inside us. When "Silent Heart Attack" returns to its theme of silence—"Silence is what you hear, / the mouth a moon of Os, black filling up / the body with its blood"—it does so by dramatizing one fusion between language and experience as a wordless ache and "a moon of Os".

Poetry often relies on the affinity between memory and metaphor, between gestation and artifice. Stanley Plumly has located this correspondence in the figure of his father, who died young. As in many of Plumly's poems that invoke the memory of his father, here his father emerges as a presence that beats "louder" in the poet's consciousness, especially as the son faces the difficult silences aching in his own hurt heart.

Not to Murder the Old

When we say that poetry is an ancient art, what we're getting at is the idea that it exists continuously in the aesthetic lanes between the old and the new, the primeval and the modern, the traditional and the avant-garde. It is charged with preserving classical forms and also with vivifying present-day idioms. It navigates between a unique literary paradox: how to fashion the traditional melodies of lyricism into the modes of everyday contemporary speech.

Poets and poetry audiences clamor for the new. We want new voices that reframe the great themes, new forms that subvert convention, and new styles that excite the senses. "Make it new," Ezra Pound demanded of poets three-quarters of a century ago, believing that "any work of art which is not a beginning, an invention, a discovery, is of little worth." But Pound didn't intend this little dictum to mean everything must be new and all that preceded it to be worthless. What he means is poets should make from the old something new and then to include the old in the new. Not to murder the old.

A question that has demanded most of my attention as a poet is this: can't you make it new and classical at once? Can you be both formal and informal simultaneously? I'm sure the answer is yes. One poet whose work exemplifies this quest is A. E. Stallings, who was born in Decatur, Georgia, in 1968, and has lived in Greece since 1999.

Stallings is the most Wilburesque poet of her generation. Her poems are elegant and witty and yet they also sublimate irony. What I mean is, they soothe and smooth emotional distress. They are alert to the good, even as they face the difficult. An Italian sonnet like "Fear of Happiness" is attractive for its simplicities. Here are the first seven lines:

Looking back, it's something I've always had:
As a kid, it was a glass-floored elevator
I crouched at the bottom of, my eyes squinched tight,
Or staircase whose gaps I was afraid I'd slip through,
Though someone always said I'd be all right—
Just don't look down or *See, it's not so bad*
(The nothing rising underfoot).

This poem says something true about fear, that it comes out of the self
("Looking back, it's something I've always had"). But as the poem
winds down, it also says something new about truth:

> Then later
> The high-dive at the pool, the tree-house perch,
> Ferris wheels, balconies, cliffs, a penthouse view,
> The merest thought of airplanes. You can call
> It a fear of heights, a horror of the deep;
> But it isn't the unfathomable fall
> That makes me giddy, makes my stomach lurch,
> It's that the ledge itself invents the leap.

Stallings's new and old argument here is that truth can also be derived
from circumstance ("the ledge itself invents the leap").

Make it new? Yes. But the new is insufficient without virtuosity
wrested from the past.

Poise

What you see everywhere these days in our little magazines and online quarterlies in early twenty-first-century America is poetry of the addled and the disheveled. Everywhere you look, cosmetic indifference, fleetingness, manufactured distress, automated irony, and rank certainty substitute for emotion, insight, and thought. American poetry has become overexcited, hesitant, misgiven, and uncertain. It's freaked out, neurotic, and uptight. It's full of distrust.

Have the new poets been overexposed to MTV? Or am I just grumpy?

A bit of both perhaps. What I'm lamenting is a radical disinterest in the idea of poetry as a dramatization of poise. Because when a poet aims for poise in her poems, she is valuing writing for the future—where the ink stays dry—and not for the benefit of an art of permanent disappearance and manufactured obsolescence.

What I'm talking about is a poet who values writing for longevity because to place one's poems into a public space is to agree to be canny. To write for longevity means to immerse one's art in the lyric values of the past in order to speak to the future. As Philip Larkin once said, poetry is a "richness" and a "release of delight" that's meant to last beyond the next news cycle and the last reader.

Phillis Levin is just this sort of poet. Since 1988, with the publication of her first book, *Temples and Fields,* she has composed poems that invoke a dazzling fusion between the ancient and the contemporary. Her brand of poetry might be called meditative—a mixture of colloquial touch, ingenious metaphors, and a mind flexible enough to fix moments onto a continuum of the sublime. In a word, her poems are poised.

"May Day" demonstrates Levin's ceremonial bearing. It begins:

> I've decided to waste my life again,
> Like I used to: get drunk on
> The light in the leaves, find a wall
> Against which something can happen,
>
> Whatever may have happened
> Long ago—let a bullet hole echoing
> The will of an executioner, a crevice
> In which a love note was hidden,
>
> Be a cell where a struggling tendril
> Utters a few spare syllables at dawn.

All of the above, from decisiveness to frivolous intent to withdrawal from modernity to recoiling into "spare" utterance, illustrates how much, as a poet, Levin understands the consequences of her ideas. The poem goes on:

> I've decided to waste my life
> In a new way, to forget whoever
>
> Touched a hair on my head, because
> It doesn't matter what came to pass,
> Only that it passed, because we repeat
> Ourselves, we repeat ourselves.

Levin dramatizes the possibilities of wasting a life in the pursuit of traveling a "long way / Out of the way." This is contrasted with an individual's experience with human "will" and "what came to pass" with a composed gravity. She's orchestrating her ideas into an assured argument. The poem concludes:

> I've decided to walk a long way
> Out of the way, to allow something
> Dreaded to waken for no good reason,
> Let it go without saying,

Let it go as it will to the place
It will go without saying: a wall
Against which a body was pressed
For no good reason, other than this.

It's worth looking closely at how this poem develops through reevaluation, reassurance, and urgency. It begins with the wall "Against which something can happen" and finally ends with the wall where a "body was pressed / For no good reason, other than this."

A poem is not about everything. A poem is about a thing. That thing is not cut off from history, nor from literary contexts, nor from influences the poet seeks through the art and through her knowledge of experience. Surely a poet will know the difference and embrace that difference in order to write a poetry of poise that uses composure and gravitas to discover and clarify.

Parallel Play

One of the things a poem does to amp up the reverb of its ideas is to change its narrative arc and emotional timbre midstream. Richard Hugo calls this maneuver "writing off the subject." When a poem shifts its directional momentum, it is erecting multidimensional layers of thought, emotion, and insight simultaneously.

Put another way, when a poem maneuvers from subject to subject, it's a lot like a trampolinist pivoting from one part of his routine to another, segueing from forward to backward to twisting without taking any extra preparatory bounces. Yes, you can identify the parts as parts but the result is an enhanced and coherent whole.

Shifting frames, sliding in and out of metaphor, and slipping from literal to figurative storylines and back illuminates cohesion in a poem's language and feeling.

One poet who has mastered these narrative acrobatics is Rodney Jones, an Alabamian poet born in 1950, whose poems cherish anecdote and place with a skeptical obsession with faith. His poem "On Pickiness" braids the domestic, the geographic, and the literary into a single astute utterance. The poem begins:

When the first mechanical picker had stripped the field,
It left such a copious white dross of disorderly wispiness
That my mother could not console herself to the waste
And insisted on having it picked over with human hands,

Though anyone could see there was not enough for ten sheets
And the hands had long since gone into the factories.

The poem has opened with a few subjects in play. There is the subject of the mother and the memory of her. There is the subject of the farm. There is the subject of collection and "waste." And there is the subject of learned experience "picked over with human hands." When the poem resumes, we are looking for the parallels to these subjects to announce themselves:

> No matter how often my father pointed this out,
> She worried it the way I've worried the extra words
>
> In poems that I conceived with the approximate
> Notion that each stanza should have the same number
> Of lines and each line the same number of syllables—
> And disregarded it, telling myself a ripple
>
> Or botch on the surface, like the stutter of a speaker,
> Is all I have to affirm the deep fluency below.
> The Hebrews distrusted Greek poetry (which embodied
> Harmony and symmetry, and, therefore, revision)
>
> Not for aesthetic reasons, but because they believed
> That to change the first words, which rose unsmelted
> From the trance, amounted to sacrilege against God.
> In countries where, because of the gross abundance
>
> Of labor, it's unlawful to import harvesting machines,
> I see the women in the fields and think of how,
> When my mother used to pick, you could tell
> Her row by the bare stalks and the scant poundage
>
> That tumbled from her sack so pristinely white
> And devoid of burrs, it seemed to have already
> Passed through the spiked mandibles of the gin.

There's a natural connection of storylines here, isn't there? The poet describes an event and his mother's response. He then cites his own behavior as owing something to the DNA of the mother's life that seems to parallel his. He keeps changing subjects and juggling parallel ideas.

Reading poetry involves locating these parallel lines. In a poem like "On Pickiness," we find stories of antiquity next to the economics of modernity, and next to that is how the larger civic story connects to the individual one Jones knows from heart. Finally, there is his mother's picking, too, which inspires Jones to return to the "pickiness" of the art of poetry:

> Dr. Williams said of Eliot that his poems were so
>
> Cautiously wrought that they seemed to come
> To us already digested in all four stomachs of the cow.
> What my father loved about my mother was not
> Just the beauty of her body and face, but the practice
>
> Of her ideas and the intelligence of her hands
> As they made the house that abides in us still
> As worry and bother, but also the perfect freedom beyond—
> As cleanliness is next to godliness but is not God.

Without debate, this poem is not about cows. It's not about modernism. And it's not about, really, poetry. Though of course it is about all these things. Stanley Plumly has written that a poem can be said to have two subjects, an announced subject and the unannounced subject or subjects. In "On Pickiness," the memory of the mother and the rescue of her values combine to be both the announced and the unannounced subjects.

And so when you are tracking a poem's parallel plays, you are trying to juggle its various investments in experience, its braid of ideas and images. And, as with watching the trampolinist, you are trying to track the sequence of parts that make up the routine of an entire poem.

A poem can be invested in multiple subjects. A poem can be invested in multiple ideas. A poem can be invested in multiple relationships. Some of these will be more dominant than others. The joy in the reading and the thrill of the writing is in keeping all the parallel parts in motion at once.

A Complicated Aftermark

When my son was in youth soccer, a mother of another player came up to me and pushed Robert Frost's "To Earthward" into my hand to ask if I would explain it to her. Not something that happens every day, but a sweet confrontation all the same.

Frost refused to read the poem in public because it was too painful and marked a deterioration in his marriage. It begins:

> Love at the lips was touch
> As sweet as I could bear;
> And once that seemed too much;
> I lived on air
>
> That crossed me from sweet things
> The flow of—was it musk
> From hidden grapevine springs
> Downhill at dusk?
>
> I had the swirl and ache
> From sprays of honeysuckle
> That when they're gathered
> Shake dew on the knuckle.

The words that come to mind to characterize the language of the opening stanzas—sexy, erotic—are words not usually associated with this famously conservative poet. But expressions of youthful ecstasy insist on their own rhetoric. Lines like "Love at the lips was touch / As sweet as I could bear" or "I had the swirl and ache / From sprays of honeysuckle" are nothing if not unambiguously carnal.

In a letter to a friend, Frost said that the poem records "one of the greatest changes my nature has undergone." I suspect he was alluding to the very "hidden" nature of a worsening relationship with his wife. Frost was working on the poem as early as 1917, when he was in his early forties, and he included it in his 1923 book *New Hampshire*, for which he received the first of four Pulitzer Prizes.

The Robert Frost in "To Earthward" is far removed from the late-in-life persona Frost played of the silver-haired, crusty, Yankee cracker barrel farmer poet. The poem continues:

> I craved strong sweets, but those
> Seemed strong when I was young;
> The petal of the rose
> It was that stung.
>
> Now no joy but lacks salt,
> That is not dashed with pain
> And weariness and fault;
> I crave the stain
>
> Of tears, the aftermark
> Of almost too much love,
> The sweet of bitter bark
> And burning clove.

The craving is nearly unbearable. The lack of joy, the omnipresent pain, the fault-finding, and the consequences of harsh words and emotions leave their stain until the poem moves to its difficult resolution:

> When stiff and sore and scarred
> I take away my hand
> From leaning on it hard
> In grass and sand,
>
> The hurt is not enough:
> I long for weight and strength
> To feel the earth as rough
> To all my length.

One of my favorite photographs of Frost is of him as a dark-haired, slender, and handsome young man. He's sitting in an armchair, writing at a makeshift desk across his lap formed by a wood plank across the chair's two arms. This is the Frost I picture behind the making of "To Earthward." It's a figure who is "stiff and sore and scarred" and longing to feel at home in the world and in the consequences of his own behavior and emotions, "To feel the earth as rough / To all my length."

Figuration—how a metaphor is performed in a poem—was of preeminent concern for Robert Frost. "The figure a poem makes," he once said, "begins in delight and ends in wisdom." He adds: "The figure is the same as for love." In "To Earthward," the rhapsodic feeling has gone sour "with pain / And weariness and fault." In the last sentence, embracing the earth, Frost practically longs for the grave.

I want to think this is what disturbed the mother of the young soccer player. We talked about it that day while watching our boys. We spoke of how a relationship can fray but the frays can be repaired, how contempt exists on the borderlines of contrition, how reproach can be buried so that regard can take its place. The closer Frost gets to the "rough" ground of his shame ("The hurt is not enough"), the more the poem seems to rise from the earth and deliver him.

"No tears for the writer, no tears for the reader," Frost is often quoted as saying, alluding to the emotional costs of being a poet. To write a poem like "To Earthward"—a poem that looks squarely at the complicated "aftermark" of a love scarred with pain—must have cost him a great deal.

A Gathering of Poets

Turbulent, fleshy, sensual, eating, drinking, and breeding...

Discovery and Definition

If there were a Top of the Pops for poetry, Robert Hayden's "Those Winter Sundays" would be on it. In a Columbia University Press survey, the poem was ranked the 266th most anthologized poem in English. This put it nearly a hundred spots ahead of "Paul Revere's Ride" (#313), but lagging behind Robert Frost's "Stopping by Woods on a Snowy Evening" (#6).

Born in 1913, Hayden grew up in a destitute African-American section of Detroit known as Paradise Valley. A neighbor's family adopted him at the age of two when his parents separated and his mother could no longer afford to keep him. His adoptive father was a strict Baptist and manual laborer. The opening of the poem illustrates how one's autobiography is the unformed stone that a poem sculpts:

> Sundays too my father got up early
> and put his clothes on in the blueblack cold,
> then with cracked hands that ached
> from labor in the weekday made
> banked fires blaze. No one ever thanked him.

Still, the new family nurtured Hayden's early literary interests, and as a teenager he was immersed in the poetry of the Harlem Renaissance and in mainstream poets such as Edna St. Vincent Millay and Carl Sandburg.

While in college, Hayden studied with the English poet W. H. Auden, who stressed a poetics of technical precision, for which Hayden was naturally suited. You can see this intelligence in the next stanza, the distracting charm of characterizing the cold, instead of the wood, as "splintering," as well as the intensification of the dramatic confrontation:

> I'd wake and hear the cold splintering, breaking.
> When the rooms were warm, he'd call,
> and slowly I would rise and dress,
> fearing the chronic angers of that house,
>
> Speaking indifferently to him,
> who had driven out the cold
> and polished my good shoes as well.

Poetic form would always remain important to Hayden. Technique, he once said, enables discovery and definition in a poem, and it provides a way of "solving the unknowns."

In 1940, Hayden published his first volume of tidy lyrics, called *Heart-Shape in the Dust*. The book drew little attention. But that would change. For the next forty years Hayden's precise style would become widely acclaimed. In 1976 he was the first African-American to serve as Consultant in Poetry to the Library of Congress, the post we now call US Poet Laureate. He died in 1980.

"Those Winter Sundays" is his heart-wrenching domestic masterpiece, and very much a poem of discovery and definition. What it discovers is a synchronicity of sound that embodies the poem's spirit of reconciliation. Listen to the K sounds: *blueblack, cracked, ached, weekday, banked, thanked, wake, breaking, call, chronic*. That percussive, consonant-cooked vocabulary is like a melodic map into how to read the poem, linking the fire, the season, the father, and his son.

Then there's what the poem defines, unspoken love. It begins with the father's for the son, when he makes the fire. Then, the unspoken love is returned at last in the poem's final two lines:

> What did I know, what did I know
> of love's austere and lonely offices?

When the adult son asks, "What did I know, what did I know...?" the tone of that repetition is more statement than question. It cuts from indifference to guilt to admiration. It's a fast moment in the poem that blossoms into the last word, "offices," a metaphor that expresses the endurance required of long-term love, of manual labor, and of the official fatherly role.

Yet it all begins with that quiet, understated opening line ("Sundays too my father got up early"), which defines Hayden's initial memory, as well as brings to mind the other unmentioned six days of the week—and for how many years?—when the father began each winter day, in the cold darkness, to warm up the home for his still-dreaming child.

Physical and Metaphysical

For the vigorous formal discipline of his free verse lines and as a master of the meditative lyric poem, Charles Wright is an exciting poet.

Born in Pickwick Dam, Tennessee, in 1935, Wright served in the Army and was stationed in Italy. There, he discovered Ezra Pound's *Pisan Cantos* and began to write his first poems. Later, he attended the Iowa Writers' Workshop, studying with Donald Justice, and took up a career in academia. Wright's earliest poems from the late sixties and seventies were tightly wound and fragmentary. By 1980, his style had opened and his books began to seem like journals of contemplative interior monologues, as you can see in the opening of "Nostalgia":

> Always it comes when we least expect it, like a wave,
> Or like a shadow of several waves,
> 　　　　　　　　　　　　one after the next,
> Becoming singular as the face
>
> Of someone who rose and fell apart at the edge of our lives.
>
> Breaks up and re-forms, breaks up, re-forms.
> And all the attendant retinue of loss foams out
> Brilliant and sea-white, then sinks away.

The poem starts by acknowledging a sentimental surge, but ends desperate to ward it off. One thing that can be said of a Charles Wright poem is that it's always in motion. His lines move impulsively from the present to the imagined, from the physical to the metaphysical, and from image to memory:

Memory's dog-teeth,
                lovely detritus smoothed out and laid up.

And always the feeling comes that it was better then,
Whatever *it* was—
                people and places, the sweet taste of things—
And this one, wave-borne and wave-washed, was part of all that.

Memory is every poet's stock and trade. "The past is the one mirror that never releases its images," Wright once said. "Layer and overlay, year after year, wherever you look, however you look, whenever you look, it's always your own face you see there."

    So what of nostalgia? Nostalgia is memory's most sugared invocation:

We take the conceit in hand, and rub it for good luck.

Or rub it against the evil eye.
And yet, when that wave appears, or that wave's shadow,
  we like it,
Or say we do,
              and hope the next time

We'll be surprised again, and returned again, despite the fact
The time will come, they say, when the weight of nostalgia,
                    that ten-foot spread

Of sand in the heart, outweighs
Whatever living existence we drop on the scales.

May it never arrive, Lord, may it never arrive.

To be nostalgic is to be in love with both the memory and the remembering. At its best, it's a form of homesickness. At its worst, nostalgia can overwhelm one's sense of being alive.

    Like memory, poems too are a recalibration of experience. What we remember in life is often a limited, even flawed, narrative of an event or feeling. Poems show us the meaning of what we might be longing for, and sometimes fearing, including the "weight" of being "surprised again, and returned again" to something we hadn't seen so well before.

Submerged into the Depths of One's Being

Consider some paradigms for a poet's life and career. There's the tragic young poet, like John Keats, who wrote for a half dozen years before dying of tuberculosis in his early twenties. There's the self-destructive poet, like Dylan Thomas, who died of alcoholism at thirty-nine, or Sylvia Plath, who killed herself. There's the late-blooming poet, like W. B. Yeats, whose mature style and achievement came after he turned sixty. There's the unknown poet, like Emily Dickinson, who published just seven poems in her lifetime, all anonymously.

Stanley Kunitz's career is a model for the journeyman poet who remains steadfast from beginning to end. Born in 1905 in Worcester, Massachusetts, Kunitz had a seventy-year career as a poet. By his late nineties, he'd outlasted—if that's the word—every poet of his generation and a few from the next, and had been awarded the National Book Award, the Pulitzer Prize, and the National Medal of Arts, and twice been appointed the Poet Laureate of the United States.

Kunitz is a poet of recall and recollection. "I think a poem lies submerged in the depths of one's being," Kunitz has said. "It's an amalgamation of images, often the key images out of a life. I think there are certain episodes in the life that really form a constellation, and that's the germinal point of the poems." The germinal event in Kunitz's life occurred a few months before he was born, when his father committed suicide by shooting himself.

Despite the title of his first book, *Intellectual Things*, published in 1930, these were poems of extreme emotion. *Intellectual Things* initiated a career of meditative, grieving, sometimes comic, other times oracular visionary poetry in the manner of William Blake. Kunitz's reputation for poems of moral gravity and mournful dignity was reaffirmed in the 1950s when he published *Selected Poems*, and again in the 1970s with his finest single volume, *The Testing-Tree*, in which "Robin Redbreast" appears.

The poem presents memory as an art of mutilation, spiritual auto-biography, and implied, intrinsic grief. First it begins with a strange observation:

> It was the dingiest bird
> you ever saw, all the color
> washed from him, as if
> he had been standing in the rain,
> friendless and stiff and cold,
> since Eden went wrong.
> In the house marked For Sale,
> where nobody made a sound,
> in the room where I lived
> with an empty page, I had heard
> the squawking of the jays
> under the wild persimmons
> tormenting him.

What is so strange about what Kunitz sees? He sees an unremarkable animal ("dingiest," "color/washed") as a contemporary outcome of the Garden of Eden's tragic flaw. And he sees it in a moment of violent transition.

Everything torments his imagination: the bird same as the house, in which he has struggled to fashion poems beyond the "empty page" and is for sale. Even the "wild persimmons." So when Kunitz moves to the next part of the poem, the unremarkable is poised to become quite remarkable and memorable:

> So I scooped him up
> after they knocked him down,
> in league with that ounce of heart
> pounding in my palm,
> that dumb beak gaping.
> Poor thing! Poor foolish life!

without sense enough to stop
running in desperate circles,
needing my lucky help
to toss him back to his element.

Now Kunitz is interested in restoring the old life. But not before he realizes that shifting back to one element from another element or a new element of experience—as in the transitions of our daily lives and the ways we recall them—is nearly impossible. Ever the journeyman, he understands that the journey is full of trials. The poem concludes:

But when I held him high,
fear clutched my hand,
for through the hole in his head,
cut whistle-clean...
through the old dried wound
between his eyes
where the hunter's brand
had tunneled out his wits...
I caught the cold flash of the blue
unappeasable sky.

The symmetry between the dingy bird and the blocked poet is hard to avoid. Both are tormented and in need. Kunitz's experience with the robin throws his life into relief and exposes the unspeakable and "unappeasable" loss.

The poem's structure, too, is typical of Kunitz's directness. The order might best be summarized as: It was the dingiest bird...I had heard its torment...So I scooped him up...Poor life...But when I held him...I caught the cold flash of truth, of epiphany, of...fill in the blank. That turn—"But when I held him"—is the poem's pivot. It epitomizes a point of discovery and illustrates its emotional remedy.

When I say that Kunitz was a journeyman poet, what I'm praising is his steadfastness such as you see here. He understands the sanctity of time. He values the art of observation. And that observation requires a poet, time and time and time again, not just to have an experience, but also to not miss or mistake the meaning of that experience.

Unconventional Utterance of Daring Thought

Emily Dickinson's life has always seemed to me to be more complex than would be suggested by the old jingle—"born in Amherst, lived in Amherst, died in Amherst"—that schoolchildren learn to recall her life of solitude.

She was born in Amherst, Massachusetts, in 1830, began writing in her twenties, and died in 1886. Her father, with whom she lived all her life, once served in Congress. That she compared him to Cromwell should tell you everything about her feelings for the old man.

Though secluded, she was not a hermetic kook. She had an active, though limited, social life. She had a great deal of correspondence, won awards in bread contests at local fairs, and suffered disastrously at love. Mostly she stayed close to her sister, brother, and their nearest friends. She knew well the works of Browning, Emerson, and Keats. In the end, she anonymously published just a handful of poems. Not until after her death was her poetry brought out in book form.

I was thinking of Dickinson one time while visiting the editorial offices of *Poetry* magazine in Chicago and thumbing through the decades of their archives. *Poetry* has been a venue for our finest poets, including T. S. Eliot, Wallace Stevens, Marianne Moore, Robert Frost, and many others, as well as outstanding poets writing today whose future influences are as yet unknown.

What struck me about those past issues is how many of the poets—for instance, Mary Blayker, Israel Kapstein, Parmenia Miguel, Josephine Pollitt, all from the 1920s—are lost to us now in the shakedown of literary values and influence. Reading their once-new poems, however, I noticed how proficient their poems are. That is to say, these poets were good at what was deemed and rewarded as being good in their day. But their poems also seem stuck outside what has become our contemporary life in poetry. That's the problem, right? They're stuck in a contemporary sound that is lost in the past.

Emily Dickinson was never proficient in this manner. She was always extraordinary.

The initial assessment of her poems by her first editors after she died—that her poetry was an "unconventional utterance of daring thoughts"—is still right on. And yet those editors smoothed out the unconventional grammar and punctuation, a disservice that later editors would correct.

Dickinson wrote some eighteen hundred poems—eccentric, enigmatic, opaque, and intensely idiosyncratic, original poems. Her influence on American poetry is incalculable. William Carlos Williams called her our "patron saint." Generations of poets have taken her as a model for the isolated poet writing poems of private experience, for the desire to turn the banal into the epiphanic, and for the composition of difficult and idiomatic rhythms, diction, and syntax.

"These are the days when Birds come back," composed in eighteen lines of irregular rhymes, is one of the few poems that Dickinson published in her lifetime:

> These are the days when Birds come back—
> A very few—a Bird or two—
> To take a backward look.
>
> These are the days when skies resume
> The old—old sophistries of June—
> A blue and gold mistake.
>
> Oh fraud that cannot cheat the Bee.
> Almost thy plausibility
> Induces my belief,
>
> Till ranks of seeds their witness bear—
> And softly thro' the altered air
> Hurries a timid leaf.

Oh sacrament of summer days,
Oh Last Communion in the Haze—
Permit a child to join—

Thy sacred emblems to partake—
Thy consecrated bread to take
And thine immortal wine!

The poem was originally titled "October" and ran in the March 1864 issue of *Drum Beat* magazine. It's a lyric rumination on that early autumn turn of New England weather known as Indian summer, with its last gasp of old and passing warmth. Each stanza contrasts the fraudulent return of summer with the cold facts of the impending winter.

"A very few—a Bird or two—" has long been one of my favorite Dickinson lines. I love the way the line's meter, with those interrupting dashes, mimics both the birds' hopping and also the way we suddenly notice the reevaluated specificity of "a Bird or two" around our consciousness.

Dickinson often invokes the figure of the child in her poems. It is, I suppose, a way of drawing us into the nature of poetry—to observe ("witness bear") with wonder and delight the mysterious and complex "emblems" of living. And it embodies the idea that poetry, at its heart, even as it wrestles with the complexities of experience, still finds inspiration and solace in qualities of innocence.

Beyond Commotions and Silences

Linda Bierds is one of our leading poets of the dramatic monologue and fictional narrative poetry. Her debut book, *Flights of the Harvest-Mare*, came out in 1985, and she has published a new book about every three years since.

Bierds, who lives on Bainbridge Island in Washington, has a gift for character—whether the characters are from photographs or paintings or about historical figures like Louis Pasteur and Amelia Earhart. Robert Frost, for instance, was terrific at dramatic monologue, too, and anyone interested in reading his best monologues would do well to begin with his poem "Home Burial."

Like Frost, Linda Bierds is attentive to poetry's central necessity of taut lines and intricate stanzas, as well as to the multiple ways in which language reveals the richness and physicality of lived experience. In a word, wordplay.

"'Will You Walk in the Fields with Me?'" involves a pistol duel and employs the kind of wordplay poets are susceptible to. It begins:

> They are matted with frost
> and a porous cloth that is the season's first snow.
> The fields. The seconds.
>
> And the firsts, of course, their manored lords.
>
> Seen from above in the dawn light, the burgundy,
> snow-dappled cloaks of the lords
> are two cardinal points of a compass,
> its jittery needle defined
> by the segmented footprints of sixteen paces.

When poets say we love the thrill of wordplay, we are talking about something like Linda Bierds's examination of the concepts of firsts and seconds in this section. The word "seconds" is the term for the men who must duel in place of the "firsts" or "manored lords." The word implies their actual and linguistic status as damaged goods, especially if one of them aims straight. And here's where the wordplay gets activated: the "seconds" are like the extra helping at a meal. They're what's left over. And, naturally, too, "seconds" indicate the segments of time in which one's life or death might be determined. And then this happens:

> It is the moment after turning. No one has fallen,
> one bullet passing through a hat brim, the other
> entering a birch tree with the sound
> of a hoof through shallow ice.
>
> At their fixed points, the lords wait. Winter wind
> sails through their cloaks. They have entered the dawn
> carrying no more than a *sense of self,* the magnetic pull
> of decorum, and stand now, smiling a little,
> satisfaction obtained by a hat brim,
>
> by a birch that shivers in the early light, as
>
> the seconds do, stomping in place in the snow.
> *They* have entered the dawn carrying, in fact,
> two bladders of salve, tourniquets browned
> by an aging sun. No selves at all, they
> are empty, waiting to be called, waiting to step forth
> in another's image—the hat plume and cloak,
>
> after his likeness, the footfalls and trembling. Waiting,
> with his grace, to make their turn,
>
> while deep in the dawn's new day, a little
> circle of darkness draws a heart-high bead
> and the beasts of the fields stand steaming.

As the poem moves through time—the seconds—it begins with the deathly image of frost on their clothing. The poem then proceeds through the miserable shootout where, prior to the winter duel's resolution, we're faced with a savage kind of human failure. And all along, time—second by second—is passing.

If reading prose fiction is the pursuit of going outside yourself into the characters and gossip of a story, then reading poetry can sometimes be more like taking a journey inward into the commotions and silences of the self. This is especially true of lyric autobiographical poetry, where the song of the self, to paraphrase Walt Whitman, is often a single voice speaking out loud more or less to no one. As readers, we overhear the lyric talk as a harmonic utterance.

But what about lyric poetry that is narrated as fiction? When we read this sort of poetry, do we read to go further into ourselves? Do we read to go outside of ourselves into the fictional drama? It's a question about the nature of poetic invocation, as well as our own expectations for reading poetry. Because even in a fictional narrative poem, we're still clearly experiencing the reading of a poem with the attendant reassuring imperatives of poetry—strong lines, swift metaphor, music, identity, strangeness, and surprise.

Magnificent Simile

There are colloquial poets, comic poets, and metaphysical poets. But few poets can match William Matthews's embodiment of all three, as when he observes "Money's not an abstraction; it's math / with consequences." Or, when speaking of children, he writes: "Our children are the only message / we can leave them."

Before his 1997 death by heart attack, at the age of fifty-five, William Matthews was also one of our most prolific poets. He published a book about every three years, as well as translations of the Roman poets Martial and Horace and the Frenchman Jean Follain.

Matthews's recurring preoccupations are embedded in a handful of his book titles: *A Happy Childhood*, *Blues If You Want*, and *Time & Money*.

You can see this mixture of the idiomatic and the witty in a poem like "Mingus at the Half Note." The poem begins with scene setting followed by an interruption:

> Two dozen bars or so into "Better Get It
> in Your Soul," the band mossy with sweat,
> May 1960 at The Half Note, the rain
> on the black streets outside
> dusted here and there by the pale pollen
> of the streetlights. Blue wreaths
> of smoke, the excited calm
> of the hip in congregation, the long
> night before us like a view and Danny
> Richmond so strung out the drums
> fizz and seethe. "Ho, hole, hode it,"

Mingus shouts, and the band clatters
to fraught silence.

Matthews demonstrates some narrative chops here. His man-on-the-
street reportage presents a poetry of location and relocation. Next,
Matthews relocates the poem from merely being a scene into being
an occasion:

There's a twinge
in the pianist's shoulder, but this time
Mingus focuses like a nozzle
his surge of imprecations on a sleek
black man bent chattering across
a table to his lavish date:
"This is your heritage and if you
don' wanna listen, then you got
someplace else you'd better be."
The poor jerk takes a few beats
to realize he'll have to leave
while we all watch before another
note gets played.

At the center of this poem is a magnificent simile. It's here, for
me, at least, that the colloquial, humorous, and metaphysical all
come together when the chastened man in the bar "glowers dimly / at
Mingus, like throwing a rock / at a cliff":

He glowers dimly
at Mingus, like throwing a rock
at a cliff, then offers his date
a disdained arm, and they leave in single
file (she's first) and don't
look back, nor at each other.
"Don't let me constrain you revelers,"
Mingus says, and then, tamed by his own rage
for now, he kick-starts the band:
"One, two, one two three four."

It's been said that a simile compares a thing to a thought or a thing
to an idea. But to get that effect, the poet must convert both—both

the thing and the thought, both the thing and the idea. Matthews adored metaphoric figuration. A quick sample: "Your heart / begins to fall like snow / inside a paperweight," or "Romantic, you could call him, / since he walks the balance beam / of his obsession like a triumphant / drunk passing a police test," or "Did we need to read / in transcript each taped word of Nixon's / contempt for us, like preserved globs of spit?"

Comparisons like these illustrate where the metaphysical really comes into play in a poem. And it's not a bad definition of poetry, either. When a metaphor alters our sense of time and space, we're in the realm of poetry.

The Gamble

One poet who has a rich understanding of the relationship between private experience and public revelation is the Polish poet Adam Zagajewski, whose poems have been appearing in English translation since the 1980s. You can see the pairing of private and public ideas in a poem like "Rome, Open City," where Zagajewski blends the intimate solace of imagination with the grand embrace of reality. First, he depicts the reality of daily time:

> A March day, the trees are still naked, plane trees patiently
> > await the leaves' green heat,
> churches caked in dust, vermillion, ocher, sienna, and bordeaux,
> > broad stains of cinnamon.

Next, his depiction of reality has to do with motivation and memory:

> *Why did we stop talking?*
> In the Barberini Palace fair Narcissus gazes at his own face,
> > lifeless.
> Brown city ceaselessly repeating: *mi dispiace.*
> Brown city, entered by weary Greek gods
> > like office workers from the provinces.

Then his depiction of reality has to do with all that impresses upon a person's consciousness:

> *Today I want to see your eyes without anger.*
> > Brown city, growing on the hills.
> Poems are short tragedies, portable, like transistor radios.

Paul lies on the ground, it's night, a torch, the smell of pitch.
Impatient glances in cafés, someone yells, a small heap of coins
    lies on the table.
    Why? Why not?
The roar of cars and scooters, hubbub of events.
    Poetry often vanishes, leaving only matchsticks.
Children run above the Tiber in funny school cloaks
    from the century's beginning:
nearby, cameras and spotlights. They're running for a film, not for
    you.
    David is ashamed of murdering Goliath.

Finally, after the realities of modern dailiness, discovered memory, and imaginative insight are rendered, Zagajewski assesses the meaning of it all. And this leads to another reality as well:

Forgive my silence. Forgive your silence.
    City full of statues; only the fountains sing.
The holidays approach, when the heathens go to church.
    Via Giula: magnolia blossoms keep their secret.
A moment of light costs just five hundred lire, which you toss
    into a black box.
We can meet on the Piazza Navona, if you want.
Matthew keeps asking himself: was I truly
    summoned to become human?

The staggeringly quiet lines quoted above combine a private version of reality with a public, mystical vision of reality, also. That's how lyric poetry bridges various realities and yet still constitutes a singular vision.

When Zagajewski asks, finally, "was I truly / summoned to become human?" he is wondering, on behalf of every poet, whether private experience can be transferred into public acceptance. That's a grubby concern—a poet's concern—having much to do with with the ambition and effect of a single poem on anyone's capacity to "become human."

Is it fair to say, then, that the act of writing and the investigation of one's imaginative life have little in the way of glamour? You scribble in a small notebook or you type onto a flaccid computer screen. You squirrel away your thoughts and stories on paper scraps. You jot down phrases on the backs of envelopes. You copy down onto moist napkins runs of dialogue overheard in a coffee shop. And you, and only you, know what you've made.

Or is it just that being a writer is a gamble? You never know if your private invocations and formulations of reality will ever be fashioned into something that others might actually read.

Epiphanies and Communion

The years between the Second World War and the Vietnam War were years of dramatic change in American poetry as we continued to shift from British models of closed metrical forms, such as rhyming sonnets and ballads, toward more avant-garde varieties of free verse.

No poet's life and career better embodies this evolution than that of the English-born poet Denise Levertov.

After she published her first book of moody, conventional poems in England in the 1940s, Levertov settled with her American husband in New York and fell under the influence of William Carlos Williams's mid-century brand of experimental plain-style writing. In her first years in the United States she began literary friendships with Robert Creeley, Robert Duncan, and Charles Olson, poets who were associated with North Carolina's Black Mountain College.

As poetic descendants of William Carlos Williams and Ezra Pound, the Black Mountain school of poets extolled openness and expressiveness in poetry rather than the use of traditional forms. A poet writes from true feelings, they argued, and out of those feelings a poem's formal shape organically emerges.

Levertov believed in open form because it more aptly expresses what she called "the sensibility of our age." Her poems from the 1950s and 1960s are models of this new American aesthetic of intense and ecstatic expression. In "O Taste and See," she praises all that lives on "the imagination's tongue," including grief, mercy, and language:

> The world is
> not with us enough.
> O taste and see

> the subway Bible poster said,
> meaning The Lord, meaning
> if anything all that lives
> to the imagination's tongue
>
> grief, mercy, language,
> tangerine, weather, to
> breathe them, bite,
> savor, chew, swallow, transform
>
> into our flesh our
> deaths, crossing the street, plum, quince,
> living in the orchard and being
>
> hungry, and plucking
> the fruit.

The result is a poet calling on herself to breathe in all of life, in-cluding to "bite, / savor, chew, swallow, transform // into our flesh our / deaths."

Levertov was born in 1923 outside London, the daughter of a Welsh mother and a Russian Jewish (turned Anglican minister) father. She was never sent to school. Instead, in a late Victorian fashion, she was given free access to her father's library. Something about that childhood play among books must have influenced her later habits. She treated poetry as both calling and daily engagement and was long concerned with what she called "the task of the poet." "The poet—when he is writing—is a priest," she once said, "the poem is a temple; epiphanies and communion take place within it."

"O Taste and See" is the title poem of her 1964 book. It represents a tough and wise kind of awareness typical of Levertov's poetry. The poem's opening lines—"The world is / not with us enough"—directly respond to William Wordsworth's 1807 sonnet "The World Is Too Much with Us, " which begins

> The world is too much with us; late and soon,
> Getting and spending, we lay waste our powers;—
> Little we see in Nature that is ours;
> We have given our hearts away, a sordid boon!

By responding to Wordsworth directly in this new manner of direct language, Levertov neatly merges her Anglo and American poetic identity. And despite the exterior differences between the two poems, Levertov, like Wordsworth, hungers for some Edenic state of mind in order to "taste and see" and pluck the "fruit" of knowledge and living.

Neither Marginalized Nor Banished

With a command so electrifying he influenced several generations of American poets (both Sylvia Plath and Anne Sexton, for instance, were his students), Robert Lowell's unparalleled achievement was wrought at great personal cost, exacerbated by a famous pedigree, annual hiatuses in mental hospitals, and a serial rebelliousness.

Lowell was born in Boston in 1917. His maternal family, the Winslows, could trace their American lineage to the *Mayflower*. His paternal family was a branch of the equally aristocratic Lowells, a Puritan clan that included a president of Harvard and the poets James Russell and Amy.

With his Boston Brahmin education predestined—first educated at St. Mark's, where he earned the nickname "Cal," short for Caligula, then at Harvard, where he did so poorly he failed to impress Robert Frost—it was a shock, in 1941, when Lowell revoked the Puritanism of his upbringing for the religion of Boston's Irish immigrants, Catholicism. He was abdicating not only a faith but what Seamus Heaney calls a "civic solidarity." Later, in his post-Catholic days, Lowell would downplay the whole business: "From zealous, atheist Calvinist to a believing Catholic is no great leap."

But the conversion was a literary catalyst nonetheless. It seemed to juice Lowell into becoming America's unrivaled Great Poet for the next thirty years. Though his struggle with depression complicated his personal life, those difficult episodes also became important material for his autobiographical style of writing. By the end of his career, Lowell had turned his manic attention exclusively to a formal and technical obsession, writing series after series of fourteen-line poems, which dominate his last three books, such as this poem, "Christmas," that begins:

> All too often now your voice is too bright;
> I always hear you . . . commonsense and tension . . .
> waking me to myself: truth, the truth, until
> things are just as if they had never been.
> *I can't tell the things we planned for you this Christmas.*
> *I've written my family not to phone today,*
> *we had to put away your photographs.*
> *We had to.* We have no choice—we, I, they? . . .

Ambiguous, innovative, and infused with American relaxation over Elizabethan decorum, Robert Lowell's six hundred-plus fourteen-line poems—sometimes he wrote several in a single sitting—have, it shouldn't surprise you to learn, an accumulative energy. Immediate and instantaneous, naturalistic and grand, their subjects include family, war, homages to poets, keepsakes, historical figures, celebrations, love, and death. The overall effect is of a poet crooning with wise sensuality, intimacy, alertness, and reminiscence. Many close readers of Lowell can't stand the fourteeners. I find their mixture of public history and confidential intimacies to be enduring.

"Christmas" comes from Lowell's 1974 book, *The Dolphin*, which centers on the dissolution of his marriage to the writer Elizabeth Hardwick. The book's enduring controversy—Lowell quoted directly from Hardwick's private letters to him—prompted his dear friend and fellow poet Elizabeth Bishop to write in a now famous letter that using Hardwick's "personal, tragic, anguished letters that way [is] cruel" and that "art isn't worth that much."

The poem's concluding lines read as follows:

> Our Christmas tree seems fallen out with nature,
> shedding to a naked cone of triggered wiring.
> This worst time is not unhappy, green sap
> still floods the arid rind, the thorny needles
> catch the drafts, as if alive—I too,
> because I waver, am counted with the living.

What I come back to again and again in this poem are a few partic-
ulars, beginning with the title that anchors the juxtaposition between
spiritual comfort and spiritual despair. Another thing I'm drawn
to is the poem's middle section that both epitomizes and exposes
Lowell's heavy state of mind ("Our Christmas tree seems fallen out
with nature, / shedding to a naked cone of triggered wiring"). The
poem is not just about Lowell. It also reveals something about the
nature of human frailty.

And the third thing comes in the last two lines of the poem: "I
too, / because I waver, am counted with the living." This writing floors
me with its pained assertion.

These passages highlight a poet's thorny predicament to not be
marginalized or banished from his own existence. Put another way:
Sometimes it helps to ask of a poem, *what hurts?* And sometimes the
answer about what hurts is a chronic ache of erasure.

Metaphor of the Whole Mind

To an American audience long infatuated with the six-and-a-half year marriage of Ted Hughes and Sylvia Plath, Ted Hughes never escaped her early characterizations of him. Besotted, she writes of Hughes, "I met the strongest man in the world, ex-Cambridge, brilliant poet whose work I loved before I met him, a large, hulky, healthy Adam... with a voice like the thunder of god." Later, she'd admire how Hughes wore "the same black sweater and corduroy jacket with pockets full of poems, fresh trout and horoscopes," calling him a "big, unruly Huckleberry Finn."

A Huckleberry Finn from the Yorkshire banks of the Mississippi River, that is.

For decades, literary critics excoriated Hughes for leaving Plath shortly before she committed suicide in 1963—"ditched" is her word—and he believed he led a sort of posthumous life afterwards where Plath was concerned.

But Plath got it right. Hughes was a presence. And he remained so in British letters for six decades, publishing over two dozen books of poetry, translations, anthologies, and essays, in addition to sixteen books for children. He was named Britain's Poet Laureate in 1984. He died in 1998.

In a review of Hughes's *Collected Poems*, Michael Hofmann calls Hughes the greatest English poet since Shakespeare. I want to agree. His poems seize a reader's nervous system. They convey and exemplify complex human images where both the psyche and the body meet.

Hughes was never interested in composing moral tales. Instead, having mastered the physical side of writing poetry early in his career, his blending of the classical with free verse form illustrates a sensation-soaked intelligence and a yearning for spiritual order. His poems unwind with an expressionistic and psychological clarity unmatched in contemporary English poetry.

Born in 1930 among the barren moors, textile mills, and stony hills of Yorkshire, Hughes grew up in the shadow of his father's disheartening World War I experience, especially his survival at the gruesome battle in Gallipoli. Although Hughes once remarked that he liked to write in hotel rooms and on trains, his poetry seldom strays from the brute harshness of his native Yorkshire. He's been called a nature poet, but he's no nature poet in a traditional British sense.

Why? Because he doesn't see the natural world as uncompromised, inextinguishable beauty or as possessing qualities of healing, or anything remotely like William Blake's conception of nature—"To see a World in a Grain of Sand / And Heaven in a Wild Flower." Instead, like the American poets he admired in his twenties, poets such as Robert Frost, Wallace Stevens, and John Crowe Ransom, Hughes sees in nature its terrifying violence and indifference to human consciousness.

Animals become stand-ins for dread and terror. Animals, he once said, contained the "deepest earliest language that my imagination learned." Such as this hawk in "Hawk Roosting":

> I sit in the top of the wood, my eyes closed.
> Inaction, no falsifying dream
> Between my hooked head and hooked feet:
> Or in sleep rehearse perfect kills and eat.
>
> The convenience of the high trees!
> The air's buoyancy and the sun's ray
> Are of advantage to me;
> And the earth's face upward for my inspection.
>
> My feet are locked upon the rough bark.
> It took the whole of Creation
> To produce my foot, my each feather:
> Now I hold Creation in my foot
>
> Or fly up, and revolve it all slowly—
> I kill where I please because it is all mine.

There is no sophistry in my body:
My manners are tearing off heads—

The allotment of death.
For the one path of my flight is direct
Through the bones of the living.
No arguments assert my right:

The sun is behind me.
Nothing has changed since I began.
My eye has permitted no change.
I am going to keep things like this.

Just listing the diction of terror and lack of consolation in these lines presents Hughes's general thesis that the natural world defies human joy or suffering. The words of defiance add up: *inaction, falsifying dream, perfect kills, rough bark, kill where I please, tearing off heads, allotment of death, no arguments, nothing has changed.* This poem illustrates the pre-Eden aura that Sylvia Plath initially found so attractive in the young Ted Hughes, doesn't it?

Hawks, crows, pikes, owls, and snakes populate Hughes's poems from his first book, *Hawk in the Rain* (1957), until his final book, *Birthday Letters* (1998). Of British poets, only D. H. Lawrence seems as drawn to animals as Hughes is, and for the same reason, for the way that they correspond to human awareness. "Every poem that works," Hughes once said, "is like a metaphor of the whole mind writing, the solution of all the oppositions and imbalances going on at that time. When the mind finds the balance of all those things and projects it, that's a poem."

"Hawk Roosting" is from his 1960 collection, *Lupercal,* and is typical of the dramatic monologues he fashioned spoken by an animal. He's said that the poem "arrived immediately" as a form of self-definition, composed in practically one sitting. For me, the poem's great rawness and alarm come in the center two stanzas, beginning with "My feet are locked upon the rough bark" until "My manners are tearing off heads."

It's here you can see how poetry can locate psychological, physical, and spiritual order. The poem is about the hawk, but really it's about us.

Knock Back Experience

Much has been written about the eighth-century Chinese poet Li Bai's weakness for the bottle and about the legend of his death, which was strange and exquisite. The rumor you hear is that, drunk in a boat, Li Bai attempted to embrace the moon's reflection and instead fell overboard and drowned.

That's certainly more romantic than the probable cause—cirrhosis of the liver. You get a fuller picture of his habit of being a poet who sacrifices life in order to write poetry in "Drinking Alone by Moonlight," translated by Tony Barnstone and Chou Ping, which begins:

> A pot of wine in the flower garden,
> but no friends drink with me.
> So I raise my cup to the bright moon
> and to my shadow, which makes us three,
> but the moon won't drink
> and my shadow just creeps about my heels.

The poor poet! His trinity of drinking companions has become his stubborn muse. When he calls for her to inspire him, she puts him on hold to fend for himself.

In truth, Li Bai's entire life during the Tang Dynasty was choked by recurring forms of rejection. Known to us also as Li Po, he was born probably in central Asia, where his family had lived in exile since the seventh century. As an adult, he was expelled for his politics from the Xian court. Briefly given amnesty, he was later arrested for treason and then banished again. He spent his last years in a quest for sympathetic patrons who were willing to support his literary ambitions.

Am I wrong to think that many readers hold the impression that ancient Chinese poems are spontaneous, delicate, and brief? That if they were jewels, they'd be pearls? Something like Li Bai's four-line poem "Summer Day in the Mountains" might be typical: "Lazy today. I wave my white feather fan. / Then I strip naked in the green forest, / untie my hatband and hang it on a stone wall. / Pine wind sprinkles my bare head."

"Song on Bringing in the Wine," on the other hand, is considerably different:

> Can't you see the Yellow River
> pours down directly from heaven?
> It sprints all the way to the ocean
> and never comes back.
> Can't you see the clear hall mirror
> is melancholy with our gray hair?
> In the morning our braids are black silk.
> In the evening they are snow.
> When happy, be happy all the way,
> never abandoning your gold cup
> empty to face the moon alone.
>
> Heaven gave me a talent. It means something.
> Born with genius, a failure now, I will succeed.
> Although I waste a thousand ounces of gold
> they will come back.
> We butcher cows, cook lambs,
> for a wild feast, and must drink
> three hundred cups at a time.
> Friends Chengfuze and Danqiuchen,
> bring in the wine
> and keep your mouths full.
> I'll sing for you. I'll turn
> your ears. Bells and drums,
> good dishes and jade are worth
> nothing. What I want
> is to be drunk, day and night,
> and never again sober up.

The ancient saints and sages are forgotten.
Only the fame of great drunks
goes from generation to generation.
In the Temple of Perfect Peace
Prince Cheng once gave a mad party,
serving ten thousand pots of wine.
Long ago. Tonight, let no one
say I am too poor to supply
vats of alcohol. I'll find
my prize horse and fur coat
and ask my boy to sell them
for fine wine. Friends, we'll drink
till the centuries
of sorrowful existence dissolve.

As you can see, the closing line is a crystallization of artistic responsi-
bility. The poem seems less about drinking than about the sacrifices a
poet makes to write poetry. A courageous Li Bai embraces the snowy
evenings. He faces "the moon alone." He is never "too poor to supply"
a fresh interpretation of experience. He always dissolves "sorrowful
existence," going "all the way to the ocean" in order to never come
back.

   You can read "Song on Bringing in the Wine" as a metaphor for
Li Bai's life and art. You can read it for the manner in which he sought
to organize his life around his art, to knock back experience and be
drunk with poetry. To believe in poetry's influence is to believe that
poetry gives meaning to life even as it expresses the inexpressible.

The Mystical, the Eternal, and the Numinous

Richard Wilbur was born in 1921 in New York City. He graduated from Amherst College, served as an infantryman during World War II, became a protégé of Robert Frost (Wilbur's wife's grandfather had been one of Frost's first editors), and published his first book of poems in 1947. Ten years later, with the publication of *Things of This World*, he won the first of two Pulitzer Prizes.

A great deal has been written about Richard Wilbur's mastery of poetic forms and measures. He possesses an artistry and musicality, to quote Anthony Hecht, that only the most "militantly tone-deaf" could fail to hear, or worse, dare to mock. I'd feel criminal not adding to the general praise. So I say to you that Richard Wilbur can bring more psychic weight to a few syllables than some poets bring to their entire oeuvre.

I bring this up, but I'm guessing, too, that Wilbur must be sick to death of hearing about it. Yes, his control is marvelous. And, yes, on account of that serene control, his meditative inclination has seldom possessed social or political urgency. In comparing him to the Irish poet Seamus Heaney, say, one wonders what Wilbur's poems would have been like had the Troubles occurred in Cummington, Massachusetts, rather than Belfast.

Wilbur is an authentic classicist to be sure. Formal, restrained, Apollonian, his poems are a "slow tongue which mumbles to in-vent / The language of the mended soul." "In Limbo," a poem from the 1980s, exhibits the Wilbur manner at once charming and impersonal. It begins:

What rattles in the dark? The blinds at Brewster?
I am a boy then, sleeping by the sea,
Unless that clank and chittering proceed
From a bent fan-blade somewhere in the room,
The air-conditioner of some hotel
To which I came too dead-beat to remember.
Let me, in any case, forget and sleep.
But listen: under my billet window, grinding
Through the shocked night of France, I surely hear
A convoy moving up, whose treads and wheels
Trouble the planking of a wooden bridge.

The iambic pentameter here is conversational and modest. And what
a fantastic pun about beating rhythms in the sixth line—"To which I
came too dead-beat to remember"—and look at that serious, mindful
echo of time in the mind with the "planking of a wooden bridge," as
well.

During a career that has lasted over sixty years, Wilbur has con-
sistently written with a metaphysical disposition about the bonds be-
tween the mundane and—a word, he said, he distrusts—the spiritual.
You can see some of this concentration in the next part of "In Limbo":

For a half-kindled mind that flares and sinks,
Damped by a slumber which may be a child's,
How to know when one is, or where? Just now
The hinged roof of the Cinema Vascello
Smokily opens, beaming to the stars
Crashed majors of a final panorma,
Or else that spume of music, wafted back
Like a girl's scarf or laughter, reaches me
In adolescence and the Jersey night,
Where a late car, tuned in to wild casinos,
Guns past the quiet house towards my desire.

When I say he has a metaphysical disposition, what I mean is that
the mind, in the act of thinking, "flares and sinks" and swirls towards
"desire." It's the idea that all external experiences carry the motion
of the intellect and the heart. It's the idea that poetry be invested in
questions of space and time, cause and effect, existence and possibility.

And it's the idea that poetry's subjects are those of the mystical, the eternal, and the numinous.

Wilbur's earliest influences were certainly poets who are concerned with discarnate questions. He has said he adored seventeenth-century English poets George Herbert, Robert Herrick, and Thomas Traherne, dramatic poets who seem to have inspired Wilbur's urbane variety of wit and Christian temperament, as follows in the next segment of the poem:

> Now I could dream that all my selves and ages,
> Pretenders to the shadowed face I wear,
> Might, in this clearing of the wits, forgetting
> Deaths and successions, parley and atone.
> It is my voice which prays it; mine replies
> With stammered passion or the speaker's pause,
> Rough banter, slogans, timid questionings—
> Oh, all my broken dialects together;
> And that slow tongue which mumbles to invent
> The language of the mended soul is breathless,
> Hearing an infant howl demand the world.

What does it mean to invent the soul? Does it mean that the soul is not natural? That the soul must be made up? Made from time, experience, DNA, history? The rest of the poem resolves the question:

> Someone is breathing. Is it I? Or is it
> Darkness conspiring in the nursery corner?
> Is there another lying here beside me?
> Have I a cherished wife of thirty years?
> Far overhead, a long susurrus, twisting
> Clockwise or counterclockwise, plunges east,
> Twin floods of air in which our flagellate cries,
> Rising from love-bed, childbed, bed of death,
> Swim toward recurrent day. And farther still,
> Couched in the void, I hear what I have heard of,
> The god who dreams us, breathing out and in.
> Out of all that I fumble for the lamp-chain.
> A room condenses and at once is true—
> Curtains, a clock, a mirror which will frame

This blinking mask the light has clapped upon me.
How quickly, when we choose to live again,
As Er once told, the cloudier knowledge passes!
I am a truant portion of the all
Misshaped by time, incorrigible desire
And dear attachment to a sleeping hand,
Who lie here on a certain day and listen
To the first birdsong, homelessly at home.

This poem illustrates what "mumbles to invent" expresses: that a voice or a mind begins in turbulence, settles like "birdsong" into a kind of glorious though difficult to comprehend voice before residing in a limbo of being "homelessly at home" in the artifice of poetry and the art of living.

With intermingling dreams, images, memories, and projections that visit us between waking and sleeping, "In Limbo" dramatizes a "clearing of the wits." The poem reveals a state of intermittent and intermediate consciousness. And it demonstrates poetry's inclination to seek out what is just beyond our reach, be it childhood, war, art, desire, death, birth, god, or, finally, even the place we call home.

Something a Poet Makes

When the British poet Philip Larkin died in 1985 at the age of sixty-three, he was probably the best-loved poet in England. Ten years later, after reaction to the controversial publication of his *Selected Letters* had set in, he was viewed as a pariah.

Outraged by Larkin's political opinions and personal behavior expressed and exposed in those letters, critics donned their moralist robes and accused Larkin of being a dour, racist Thatcherite, a self-abusing misogynist, and a porn addict. Some advocated the banning of his books.

Martin Amis, the writer and son of Larkin's oldest friend, the novelist Kingsley Amis, wrote a couple of pieces to defend Larkin's poetry and summarized the state of affairs in Larkin criticism: "The word 'Larkinesque' used to evoke the wistful, the provincial, the crepuscular, the unloved. Now it evokes the scabrous and the supremacist. The word 'Larkinism' used to stand for a certain sort of staid, decent, wary Englishness. Now it refers to the articulate far right."

Larkin hadn't changed. Neither had his poems. But the public, drunk on 1990s politically correct elixir, had.

When the character assault on Larkin heated up, I was dismayed. Certainly readers knew his misanthropic poems beforehand. Didn't they realize that Larkin understood exactly who he was, even accusing himself in the poem "Posterity" of being an "old-type *natural* fouled-up" guy? When a poet writes "Man hands on misery to man. / It deepens like a coastal shelf," you've got to conclude he's no optimist about humanity. He might even dislike people.

One question to ask is, how much should we care whether a poet has a bitter disposition or an ugly world view in his private life or private letters? All things considered, I say not much. Sure, we should care. But we should do so in balance with the importance of the body of writing. The poems, not the saintly or seedy life of the poet who wrote them, is what I want to care about. A poem is something a poet makes; it's not the life he lives. It's a judgment call every reader is faced with.

This is the sort of question Larkin faces in "I Remember, I Remember." Like readers of an unpleasant poet, he too feels weariness when confronted with the actual complexities of life. Specifically he feels weariness around his childhood, which in turn leads him to confront his own mortality—one of his favorite themes. The poem opens with a surprising discovery during an average train ride:

> Coming up England by a different line
> For once, early in the cold new year,
> We stopped, and, watching men with number-plates
> Sprint down the platform to familiar gates,
> "Why, Coventry!" I exclaimed. "I was born here."

That "Why" says a lot, doesn't it? It's part exclamation and part interrogation, as in why here, and why not somewhere else? As in, what is it about here that makes this poet who he is? Larkin's principal method of meditation is to intensify patterns of rediscovery. It goes like this: now that he's noticed the place outside the train, he leans out to look at it again with fresh eyes. You see this same meditative approach in Larkin's great poems "Church Going" and "The Whitsun Weddings." His vantage is followed by a re-vantage. And this approach to thinking is what might be called Larkinesque:

> I leant far out, and squinnied for a sign
> That this was still the town that had been "mine"
> So long, but found I wasn't even clear
> Which side was which. From where those cycle-crates
> Were standing, had we annually departed
>
> For all those family hols? ... A whistle went:
> Things moved. I sat back, staring at my boots.
> "Was that," my friend smiled, "where you 'have your roots'?"

No, only where my childhood was unspent,
I wanted to retort, just where I started:

Another poet might have let it go there. But Larkin is just revving
up. He's partly lost ("Which side was which") and partly he recognizes
that he had found himself long, long before. This self-awareness leads
him to conclude that his early life was "unspent." And then Larkin
does the poet's thing. He re-invents what isn't there:

By now I've got the whole place clearly charted.
Our garden, first: where I did not invent
Blinding theories of flowers and fruits,
And wasn't spoken to by an old hat.
And here we have that splendid family

I never ran to when I got depressed,
The boys all biceps and the girls all chest,
Their comic Ford, their farm where I could be
"Really myself." I'll show you, come to that,
The bracken where I never trembling sat,

Determined to go through with it; where she
Lay back, and "all became a burning mist."
And, in those offices, my doggerel
Was not set up in blunt ten-point, nor read
By a distinguished cousin of the mayor,

Who didn't call and tell my father *There
Before us, had we the gift to see ahead*—
"You look as if you wished the place in Hell,"
My friend said, "judging from your face." "Oh well,
I suppose it's not the place's fault," I said.

"Nothing, like something, happens anywhere."

Larkin once said that what he most remembered of his childhood was
the feeling of boredom. He couldn't wait to grow up. You could say
he was an old man at a very young age. "I Remember..." was written
in 1954 when he was thirty-one—and the last line is one of the most

crushing self-assessments he ever wrote in a career of crushing self-assessment.

"I Remember..." is an example of poetry's compositional calling: notice something, mis-know it, reconsider it, then assess it anew. The devastation of the poem's last line is like a coffin lid coming down. And yet, there's a dim light of optimism, too. That's another of poetry's compositional tasks: to determine what's true inside what is also ambiguous. And that also is the problem readers face when reading a poet whose private life we might not find to our liking.

Comfort and Sanctity

In 8 AD, the poet Publius Ovidius Naso, known as Ovid, was exiled from Rome by Emperor Augustus Caesar to the town of Tomis, near the Danube River, in what is now Romania. The reasons for his banishment have remained something of a literary mystery, though it's generally thought that he offended the Emperor's prudish tastes upon the publication of *The Art of Love*, a collection of erotic poems.

Literary exile is a form of psychic claustrophobia accompanied by marching in place. The exiled poet belongs in two places and nowhere at the same time. Fiercely dedicated to the comfort and sanctity of his art, the exiled poet writes less in solitude, which is to be valued, but more in isolation. On the one hand, he struggles with intense ennui. On the other hand, his mind is tangled in the frontiers of near-madness.

The history of exiled poets is long: Dante banished from Florence, Osip Mandelstam thrown into Soviet work camps, Pablo Neruda smuggled out of Chile, Czeslaw Milosz sequestered from Poland to California. Before them all was Ovid, who desperately hoped that his book-length poem *Tristia* would convince someone in Rome to advocate for his return. It didn't. He died alone in Tomis in 17 AD.

While Ovid's *Metamorphosis* is one of Western literature's grand masterpieces, his *Tristia* is less known, often classified as a noteworthy poem under the category of the literature of exile. I've always admired Ovid's humanistic stance in the poem: courageously addressing his political predicament, frank about his personal isolation, and eloquent about his fear of emotional and compositional debilitation:

> I'm falling apart, ramshackle, dilapidating to ruin
> cracks crazing what's left of my façade.
> In any decent neighborhood, I should be a disgrace...
> There's nothing for it, no way out...

The lines I've quoted are excerpts from Book V of *Tristia*, from a laissez-faire translation by David R. Slavitt. Ovid grows exhausted with self-pity, denounces Tomis as a provincial backwater, fears he's losing his mother tongue of Latin, and finds faith in poetry as representing all that remains from his former life. Darkly, he characterizes the exiled poet's fierce urgent calling as, unquestionably, a "hell of a life." It's an existence that confirms Aeschylus's point about "how men in exile feed on dreams."

If writing poems is a means to overcome displacement, exclusion, even relegation, and if reading poetry accomplishes a similar objective, then the art of poetry becomes a means to share messages from one exiled imagination to another. Because exile, as Mahmoud Darwish has said, "is more than a geographical concept." Just reading poetry can give you the feeling, gloriously, of being an exile of the mind and the heart, quoting Darwish again, "in your homeland, in your own house, in a room."

The Crime of Writing a Poem

In the spring of 1934, while entertaining his wife and some friends in his Moscow living room, Osip Mandelstam recited one of his unpublished poems. The poem describes the Soviet dictator Joseph Stalin as brutal and non-human—non-human because he was Georgian ("Ossetian") and not Russian. Here it is in Robert Tracy's translation:

We live, but we do not feel the land beneath us;
Ten steps away and our words cannot be heard,

And when there are just enough people for half a dialogue—
Then they remember the Kremlin mountaineer.

His fat fingers are slimy, like slugs,
And his words are absolute, like grocers' weights.

His cockroach whiskers are laughing,
And his boot-tops shine.

He has a rabble of skinny-necked leaders around him,
He plays games with the aid of those who are only half human,

Who twitter, who mew, who whimper.
He alone bangs and thrusts.

Decree after decree, he hammers them out like horseshoes—
One in the groin for him, in the forehead for him, for him one over
   the eyes, one in the eyes for him.

When he has an execution, it's a special treat
And the Ossetian chest swells.

As I say, this was an unpublished poem. A few days later one of Mandelstam's guests alerted the authorities to the existence of the poem and Mandelstam was suddenly at risk of arrest. This is not the kind of trouble most American poets are likely to experience. We are seldom concerned with the government censoring our poems.

The aim of censorship is to force writers and poets—and citizens generally—to conform their opinions, beliefs, and values to some official ideology. Or at least to be cowered enough to stay quiet about it. What censors always claim they do is enforce virtue. But it's a bogus and faulty virtue. Censorship prohibits independent thought and imaginative inventiveness. When officials believe that the political, social, or moral order is threatened, they act to restrict free expression.

That's the nasty clamp Mandelstam got caught in. Once betrayed, he was quickly arrested for what can only be called the crime of writing a poem. His papers were confiscated and then he was sentenced to hard labor on the White Sea Canal, one of the more brutal Soviet work camps. It's worth noting, ironically, sadly, though not surprisingly, his informer was arrested not long after Mandelstam was and later died in a concentration camp.

Mandelstam's cause was aided by writers favored by the Kremlin and he was soon released from the White Sea Canal and exiled to Voronezh in southwest Russia near the Ukrainian border. Destitute and homeless, he saw his exile ended in 1937. Then, in 1938, he was re-arrested and sentenced to five years hard labor near Vladivostok. The last time he was seen, he was picking at garbage in search of something to eat. He died shortly thereafter.

That's arrested, sentenced, exiled, and then essentially executed for writing a poem he never published. Anyone who wants to read about the crushing effects of literary censorship amid the politics of the Soviet period will want to read Nadezhda Mandelstam's heartbreaking memoir *Hope Against Hope*, about her efforts to free her husband from penal servitude.

When I think of Osip Mandelstam, I'm convinced that writing poetry is always a subversive activity—that all activities of the imagination are subversive. And I have to ask: why is it that so few people seem to understand this fact? Because political tyrants certainly do.

Put another way: as Mandelstam laments, for a dictator "an execution, it's a special treat."

Imposing limits on artistic expression is not much different from putting limits on who one can talk to without fear of being monitored or failing to impose limits on violence during interrogations. Censorship is intimidation with a human face. Every poet and every reader of poetry would do well to think deeply about the burdens of writing poems.

As for Mandelstam, it wasn't until the 1970s that his poems were allowed to appear in the Soviet Union, and then mostly for international sale abroad. Today, in Russia, they are at last widely available.

What is at stake when a person writes a poem? One thing is a quest to record the existence of one's living life and also one's life of the imagination. Poetry is an imprint both of a single mind and also all of human consciousness. Poetry matters because it's the art of the very medium—language—of our daily discourse. By using the means by which we say the most basic things—such as "I'm hungry, I fear, I love"—a poet understands that the imagination is the touchstone for thinking and speaking and writing without fear of reprisal or vengeance.

Uninterested in Certainty

May Swenson was born in Logan, Utah, in 1913, spoke Swedish in her childhood home, attended college at Utah State University, and then moved to the East Coast where she lived mostly in New York City until her death in 1989.

Swenson has a tender, almost rapturous sensibility. In the broadest sense her work is about ardor. Her passion is for colors and odors, for seasons and sunlight, for fireflies, frogs, tides, wishes, shadows, danger, men, women, and discreet treasures of time. Though she was a religious skeptic, Swenson's voice contains a wonderful incarnation of a divine-seeking sort of spirituality:

Body my house
my horse my hound
what will I do
when you are fallen

Where will I sleep
How will I ride
What will I hunt

Where can I go
without my mount
all eager and quick
How will I know
in thicket ahead
is danger or treasure
when Body my good
bright dog is dead

How will it be
to lie in the sky
without roof or door
and wind for an eye

With cloud for shift
how will I hide?

Framed as an invocation, this poem, "Question," raises a question about the differences and similarities between poetry and prayer. It's been said that poems are like prayers. I disagree. Poems can connote ritual or adhere to tradition. They can affirm faith or imply it. And they can address the celestial along with the terrestrial.

But a poem is not, in the end, a prayer, because poetry is unaffiliated.

While prayer unites private faith with public affirmation and seeks communion between the petitioner and God, poetry seeks communion among the poet, the poets of the present and the past, and a community of readers. These characteristics don't cancel each other out, mind you. But they are different.

I wouldn't suggest that you cling too slavishly to such distinctions. As Harold Bloom writes in the introduction to his anthology *American Religious Poems*, any distinction "between sacred and secular literature is finally a political judgment, and therefore irrelevant in the realms of the aesthetic." Though I sometimes get the numbering mixed up between the Biblical Psalms and Shakespeare's sonnets, "The Lord is my shepherd I shall not want" (Psalm 23) is definitively prayerful while "That time of year thou mayst in me behold" (Sonnet 73) is definitely not.

May Swenson's poems are deeply connected to the long tradition of this country's religious poetry. American religious poetry begins with the work of Protestant colonials like Anne Bradstreet, steers toward a nineteenth-century communion with the visible forms of nature in the poems of, say, William Cullen Bryant or the passionless hymns of Ralph Waldo Emerson, then glides into the pinnacle of the nineteenth century where divine expression takes a surprising lyric turn toward the inwardly visionary with Walt Whitman's god of the self and what Bloom calls Emily Dickinson's "sect of one."

Throughout the twentieth century—whether it was Robinson Jeffers's embrace of a deified watery Pacific Ocean or Wallace Stevens's god of mere being or Elizabeth Bishop's unbelieving seizures of epiphany or James Wright's instantaneous breakage into blossom—spiritual awakening in American poetry has cut a path between the literal and the figurative. These days there are plenty of poets of religious affiliations writing important poems of faith as well.

May Swenson concentrates on the tensions of this crossroad. "Question" doesn't attempt to answer Swenson's question because the poem is uninterested in certainty. Instead, the poem is an ecumenical exultation. Its premise, like the premise of all poetry, is with asking—but perhaps not offering answers—about the relationships between blood and flesh, and mystery and mysticism.

Something Uncoerced

Few poets have been as influential in the world of twentieth-century poetry as Anna Akhmatova, the diva of Russia's Silver Age, who died in 1966 at the age of seventy-six. Since she published her first book, *Evening*, in 1912, Akhmatova's gracious and reticent poems have almost single-handedly taught generations of poets how to write about erotic love, political defiance, and individual dignity.

Akhamatova's protégé, the Russian Nobel laureate Joseph Brodsky, once said of her that she "is the kind of poet that simply 'happens'; that arrives in the world with an already established diction and his/her own unique sensibility. She came fully equipped, and she never resembled anyone." The poet in American poetry this description most reminds me of is Emily Dickinson, whose imitators, like Akhmatova's, consistently fail to produce a similar music, and instead, as Brodsky says, "end up resembling one another more than her."

A stunning beauty, Akhamatova was widely sketched, painted, photographed, and swooned over. But she suffered as other Russians did against the molestations of Stalinist tyranny. Her close friends were sent to prison, as was her husband. And her son spent eighteen years in labor camps, during which time Akhmatova, desperate for his release, agreed to write patriotic poems which were then disseminated internationally to prove that she was alive and, well, let's say writing fervently.

The poems that mattered to her most during this period—from the 1930s to the 1950s—she refused to write down at all. Instead, as with the poem "Native Soil," she memorized them or had friends memorize them, and then they would privately recite them back to her so she could be certain that she had, in fact, made something new in the world, something uncoerced, and that her true literary life still existed, as this English rendition by D. M. Thomas shows:

> Our hearts don't wear it as an amulet,
> It doesn't sob beneath the poet's hand,
> Nor irritate the wounds we can't forget
> In our bitter sleep. It's not the Promised Land.
> Our souls don't calculate its worth
> As a commodity to be sold and bought;
> Sick, and poor, and silent on this earth,
> Often we don't give it a thought.
>> Yes, for us it's the dirt on our galoshes,
>> Yes, for us it's the grit between our teeth.
>> Dust, and we grind and crumble and crush it,
>> The gentle and unimplicated earth.
> But we'll lie in it, become its weeds and flowers,
> So unembarrassedly we call it—ours.

Christian Wiman has written that great poetry comes when a "fully inhabited life—be it brief, or narrow, or in some fundamental way thwarted—has been suffered into form." Akhmatova's best poems have this anguish behind them. If there's some truth to the idea that all poetry is either love poetry or political poetry, or both, and I believe that's generally so, then at her best, Akhmatova's political poems are typically and uniquely charged with erotic undercurrents. They're certainly not partisan. They're seldom nationalistic.

Brodsky again: "At certain periods of history it is only poetry that is capable of dealing with reality by condensing it into something graspable, something that otherwise couldn't be retained by the mind. In that sense, the whole nation took up the pen name Akhmatova."

A poem like "Native Soil" looks past governments and politics, laws and legislation, in order to reveal the *terra firma* that draws a people together.

Walking Out on the Walkout

Here's something I never thought I'd write. Once I gave a lecture about Allen Ginsberg's iconic poem "Howl" to seventy undergraduates when a handful of them up and walked out on me. I was later told they objected to the poem's foul language and mentions of sex.

Foul language and mentions of sex offending college students!

True, this Cold War-era poem is frank about homosexuality, drugs, pacifism, and industrial violence. True, when *Howl and Other Poems* was published in 1956 in San Francisco, the bookseller was arrested and accused of intent to selling lewd literature. But the obscenity trial went nowhere. Judge Clayton Horn ruled that the poem was not obscene and he prevented it from being censured. While the poem became an emblem of the Beat generation, Ginsberg went on to have an international career as an American troubadour until his death in 1997. The poem is now standard curricula in universities throughout the world, including the five military academies of the United States.

Little of the poem ought to be shocking today. I mean: we live in the world "Howl" created. Sexual freedom is a cultural cornerstone, notwithstanding the AIDS epidemic or debates about contraception that might make you wonder if we're not still living in the fifties—the 1750s, I mean. Same-sex marriage is permitted in over three dozen states and counting. Marijuana has been decriminalized in a dozen more states. The UN Commission on Human Rights in 1995 reaffirmed the rights of pacifists. Around the world capitalism still has detractors.

Yes, we live in the world that "Howl" created.

So consider me shocked when a few students stormed out of the lecture hall. Shocked, I say, because if the poem's dirty language sent them to their dorm rooms to enjoy their cleanliness, and if they ended up cowering and "listening to the Terror through the wall," they're Ginsbergians through and through.

Meanwhile, I can report that many of the remaining students loved the poem—as so many young people have for generations. They admire the courage it must have taken Ginsberg to write boldly against American conformity. And to write so memorably, as in the famous opening three lines:

> I saw the best minds of my generation destroyed by madness,
>   starving hysterical naked,
> dragging themselves through the negro streets at dawn looking
>   for an angry fix,
> angelheaded hipsters burning for the ancient heavenly connection
>   to the starry dynamo in the machinery of night

Here Ginsberg is ditching hushed elegance in favor of framing an argument. Yes, even if it requires using crude language.

But now here are the delicate, tender, final lines of the poem, in which Ginsberg welcomes his troubled friend, Carl Solomon, into safety:

> I'm with you in Rockland
>   where we hug and kiss the United States under our bedsheets
>   the United States that coughs all night and won't let us sleep
> I'm with you in Rockland
>   where we wake up electrified out of the coma by our own souls'
>   airplanes roaring over the roof they've come to drop angelic bombs
>   the hospital illuminates itself imaginary walls collapse O skinny
>   legions run outside O starry-spangled shock of mercy the eternal
>   war is here O victory forget your underwear we're free
> I'm with you in Rockland
>   in my dreams you walk dripping from a sea-journey on the
>   highway across America in tears to the door of my cottage in the
>   Western night.

As a traditional lament, "Howl" bemoans the destruction of youth, deplores the violence caused by industrial civilization, and suffers for

the wounded life of Carl Solomon, whom Ginsberg met in a psychi-
atric hospital in the late 1940s. Through a complex set of metaphors,
Ginsberg makes a sustained argument that the violence of American
culture and industry poisons the sanctity of the imagination. It pushes
individuals—gays, pacifists, free spirits—to the fringes. Then that
same culture accuses the vulnerable outcasts of being undisciplined
reprobates who live beyond the mainstream.

But this poem, as poetry must, widens the very ideal of what
mainstream means and articulates an inclusive vision of humanity.
It epitomizes poetry's capacity to include the minute and the global.
It pays attention to the particulars of existence. And it refreshes our
thoughts and feeling about the world we all share.

Two Eternities

Every autumn from 2007 to 2011 I commuted from Portland to Winston-Salem, North Carolina, where the weather would be in the thick of that city's late-summer humidity. The trees would be sagging and over-burdened and wiped out. The light spilled with just-around-the-horizon anticipation of some other season that was as yet impossible to imagine. Crickets crying at dusk seemed to be nesting inside my head.

In that weather, almost automatically, I would find myself thinking of North Carolina's native son, A. R. Ammons. He was born in rural North Carolina in 1926—and, by coincidence, we share the same birthday. He arrived on the campus of Wake Forest University in the late 1940s, fresh from serving on a navy destroyer during World War II. It was at Wake that he began to write poems, while taking a degree in science. The minute observations and grand reflections in his poetry for the next five decades must owe something to his early studies in deductive reasoning.

With meticulous attention to both the seen and the unseen, with a tone that combines scrutinizing self-knowledge with backdoor whimsy, Ammons, who died in 2001, has been one of the most transcendental poets in contemporary American poetry.

I mean, he just seems to trip over epiphanies. His writing is sincere, analytic, and radiant, as in these lines from his poem "Hymn":

> And I know if I find you I will have to stay with the earth
> inspecting with thin tools and ground eyes
> trusting the microvilli sporangia and simplest coelenterates
> and praying for a nerve cell
> with all the soul of my chemical reactions
> and going right on down where the eye sees only traces

This is an example of not just noticing, but poring over the natural world. Writing like this reveals a mind fascinated both by ideas and how ideas get processed through experience and language. Same goes with the following poem, "Cut the Grass," on a similar theme:

> The wonderful workings of the world: wonderful,
> wonderful: I'm surprised half the time:
> ground up fine, I puff if a pebble stirs:
>
> I'm nervous: my morality's intricate: if
> a squash blossom dies, I feel withered as a stained
> zucchini and blame my nature: and
>
> when grassblades flop to the little red-ant
> queens burring around trying to get aloft, I blame
> my not keeping the grass short, stubble
>
> firm: well, I learn a lot of useless stuff, meant
> to be ignored: like when the sun sinking in the
> west glares a plane invisible, I think how much
>
> revelation concealment necessitates: and then I
> think of the ocean, multiple to a blinding
> oneness and realize that only total expression
>
> expresses hiding: I'll have to say everything
> to take on the roundness and withdrawal of the deep dark:
> less than total is a bucketful of radiant toys.

When you read these lines closely, you may come to believe that Ammons would have agreed with Henry Thoreau, who once said that the relationship between the human being and the natural world is a dance between "two eternities," adding that "happiness or change or growth" can occur only by living in the present moment.

Here's Ammons on a similar theme: "I think how much / revelation concealment necessitates"—as if to say that the self is a vessel of many selves united first by intuition and then by the desire to understand how the entirety of the inner life transcends the physical world.

Isn't that a fine characterization of poetry's best ambition? To unconceal revelation?

Affirmation

And join thy voice unto the angel quire...

A Secret Self

Because poetry has so little remunerative allure, it can sometimes seem that poets are overly concerned with writing for immortality. I suspect that readers distrust this sort of ambition. And yet I'm surprised by this distrust, too, because I think many readers of poetry have at least one poem close to their hearts, a poem that has special and intimate importance to you.

Still, people mistrust poetry. Dylan Thomas faces the question at the beginning of his poem "In My Craft or Sullen Art," which begins:

> In my craft or sullen art
> Exercised in the still night
> When only the moon rages
> And the lovers lie abed
> With all their griefs in their arms,
> I labor by singing light
> Not for ambition or bread
> Or the strut and trade of charms
> On the ivory stages
> But for the common wages
> Of their most secret heart.

What does it mean to write for the "common wages" of our "most secret heart" anyway? Does this ambition divide and create animosity between poet and reader? Perhaps.

One reason for the mistrust between poet and reader must have something to do with the idea, as Thomas suggests, that to write a poem is to invest, to one degree or another, in a secret self. Anton

Chekhov takes the point further, arguing that the "personal life of every individual is based on secrecy."

You can see how a reader might feel put off, or at least skittish, about the machinations of someone else's secret imagination, and then, as a consequence, come to label everything having to do with poetry as at best allusive and at worst pretentious.

One person linked with this sort of antagonism toward poetry was Plato, who was so suspicious of Athenian poets he wanted them banned from his ideal Republic.

You might ask, what was Plato's beef with the poets anyway?

For one thing, he felt that poetry should primarily serve morality. He considered poems that are interested only in imitating beauty and nature—or that pay no heed to deities—to be decadent and socially corrupt. If poetry "knows nothing of true existence," Plato argues, then it must be about appearances only. Poems, he felt, ought to idealize the world. Otherwise the whole business is just a triviality. Above all, for Plato, to write or to read poetry wasn't just to be anti-social. It was to be subversive.

Well, hold on, my ancient Greek friend. That's a subversion we can't do without, because poetry, like all art, clarifies and electrifies the private emotional life of both the poet and the community of readers.

I've been thinking recently about some lines I love by W. H. Auden from his poem "Lullaby," which read:

> Lay your sleeping head, my love,
> Human on my faithless arm;
> Time and fevers burn away
> Individual beauty from
> Thoughtful children, and the grave
> Proves the child ephemeral:
> But in my arms till break of day
> Let the living creature lie,
> Mortal, guilty, but to me
> The entirely beautiful.

As emotional signposts, these lines dramatize the gray zone between love and guilt. They clarify something about the fleetingness of existence and make a stand for what life, and by extension, love is. The whole idea here is something daring and precious. Yet even while a poet has no control over what a reader privately thinks when reading his poems, there is certainly poetry's "singing light."

You see something of this in the way Thomas figures the conclusion of "In My Craft or Sullen Art":

> Not for the proud man apart
> From the raging moon I write
> On these spindrift pages
> Nor for the towering dead
> With their nightingales and psalms
> But for the lovers, their arms
> Round the griefs of the ages,
> Who pay no praise or wages
> Nor heed my craft or art.

Thomas's light provides a means for the emotions of our lives to exist in the living world. He makes a wonderful stand for poetry's endurance, even as he owns up to the public's ambivalence, indifference, and opposition to it. That sort of opposition must be overcome in every poem. And that's why Thomas makes a stand for poetry's ambition to be an art "for the lovers, their arms / Round the griefs of the ages."

Swooning v. Stinginess

All the rage for some American poets these days is employing semiotic linguistic theories as the compositional basis for writing. By doing so, these poets would tell you, they are writing toward a theoretical poetics that makes their poems truer to human thought.

Sure, OK. Speaking for myself, I also want poems to make me feel something.

This debate between ideas and emotions is a long-standing one among poets. A poet hopes his poems "teach or please" or both, wrote the ninth-century-BC Roman poet Horace, who also posited that when poets get too "lofty, they commence" with a "purple patch of cheap magnificence."

I suspect a good reader of poetry naturally feels that poetry is supposed to please and delight and also have the urgency of language and life. But, as my semiotic friends suggest, somewhere between the Renaissance swooning of, say, John Suckling, and the Modernist stinginess of, say, William Carlos Williams, poets have recoiled from the notion that delight is central to their work. Instead, these poets want lines and stanzas of intricate linguistic theorems to be the dominant characteristic of their poems.

I over-generalize. But we've traveled pretty far from the opening four lines of Suckling's song "Out upon it, I have lov'd":

> Out upon it, I have lov'd
>   Three whole days together;
> And am like to love three more,
>   If it prove fair weather.

Still, a poetry of delight does flourish in certain corners of contemporary American poetry. One poet who especially embraces language's sweeter ambiguities is Richard Kenney of Port Townsend, Washington. Kenney, who was born in 1948 in upstate New York, composes with a unique emotional, musical, and intellectual braid. There are times I think no one, and I mean no one, writes like him. Mixing formality, surprise, intelligence, and emotional heft, his poems can be decorous and ribald, moral and subversive, intricate and accessible, analytic and intuitive.

Here are some lines that contain a wry Y2-K lament cushioned with a concluding punch line of swooning self-deprecation:

> I wish for no cars, coalfires, clang-
> Clang nuclear alarms, or only electric motors
> For the Great Mother, and we had ten-speed recycling
> And aquaculture bars, and the great circle
> Closed again, and golden eagles eagling.
> Wouldn't it be great if jobs were sweaty and outdoors
> And people lived so simply nothing was lacking?
> Wouldn't it be perfect if every man could hammer
> His own nail and every woman hem
> Her own hem? And vice versa? And backpacking.
> Wouldn't it be better if we could just live in harmony
> With our own energy, and with nature's millennial rhythm?
> Oh, wouldn't it be grand if there weren't too many
> People in the world, and I was one of them?

When you read these lines, you can see how Kenney seems not just to adore but to revere language's capacity for ambiguity. At the root of this aesthetic is an interest in clarity and velocity. In his little *ars poetica* "Poetry," Kenney demonstrates what fast looks like in a poem:

> Nobody at any rate reads it much. Your
> lay
> citizenry have other forms of fun.
>
> Still, who would wish to live in a culture
> of which future anthropologists would say
> *Oddly, they had none?*

Or, here, from the opening of his poem "Pathetic Fallacy":

> The rocks look wrinkled
> and the sea, sore
>
> and what do the willows
> know of war?
>
> The king in his orchard
> curdles noon
>
> till the stars are salt
> in the western wound.

What do you get from this kind of whip-smart, clarifying poetics? You get the following. Ideas leap toward emotions. Images quicken into thoughts. Consonants and vowels are put in service of delight and insight. All to give you an accessible emotional ride.

No, this is not poetry of semiotics and harmonics. This is a seminal poetry of human harmony.

Not the Barometer That
Changes the Weather

Poets love to define poetry. And because poetry is so difficult to define, the definitions tend to be allusive and ambiguous and wonderfully alluring.

"Poetry is what gets lost in translation," is how Robert Frost puts it.

"Poetry is a mirror which makes beautiful that which is distorted," Percy Shelley says.

"Poetry is a packsack of invisible keepsakes," Carl Sandburg writes.

"Breathe in experience," Muriel Rukeyser says, and then "breathe out poetry."

Even Sigmund Freud, though not a poet, gets into the act: "Everywhere I go, I find a poet has got there before me."

A poet who seems to have gotten there before many others is the influential Polish minimalist Zbigniew Herbert (1924–1998), whose defiance against Nazism and Stalinism made him an international favorite in the West after the Second World War.

His poem, "I Would Like to Describe," for instance, begins:

> I would like to describe the simplest emotion
> joy or sadness
> but not as others do
> reaching for shafts of rain or sun
>
> I would like to describe a light
> which is being born in me

> but I know it does not resemble
> any star
> for it is not so bright
> not so pure
> and is uncertain
>
> I would like to describe courage
> without dragging behind me a dusty lion
> and also anxiety
> without shaking a glass full of water

Unlike other Eastern European poets who found their subjects in political resistance, Herbert didn't craft poems with public rhetoric in mind. What I mean is, he's not describing the "simplest" totalitarianism but the "simplest emotion."

At the same time, as these next lines show, he is exposing tyranny. In a voice that holds a quiet morality, he clarifies existence in neither programmatic nor hysterical terms:

> to put it another way
> I would give all metaphors
> in return for one word
> drawn out of my breast like a rib
> for one word
> contained within the boundaries
> of my skin
>
> but apparently this is not possible
>
> and just to say—I love
> I run around like mad
> picking up handfuls of birds
> and my tenderness
> which after all is not made of water
> asks the water for a face
> and anger
> different from fire
> borrows from it
> a loquacious tongue

so is blurred
so is blurred
in me
what white-haired gentlemen
separated once and for all
and said
this is the subject
and this is the object

In some ways, writing like this appears almost without intensity. The poem, in this translation by Czeslaw Milosz and Peter Dale Scott, accrues its argument by presenting one man's resilient humanity against the state of authoritarianism's unreal dogma: "I run around like mad / picking up handfuls of birds / and my tenderness / which after all is not made of water / asks the water for a face." Lines like these show Herbert to be biased in favor of authentic expressions of argument and not mere symbolic political argument.

A poet, said Herbert, is a "partisan of the truth...who brings everything into question." This may be true. But Herbert also knew that a poet's threat to political order is seldom complete: "It is vanity to think that one can influence the course of history by writing poetry. It is not the barometer that changes the weather."

With that in mind, you can read the conclusion of "I Would Like to Describe" as a lament:

we fall asleep
with one hand under our head
and with the other in a mound of planets

our feet abandon us
and taste the earth
with their tiny roots
which next morning
we tear out painfully

Has what a poet faces in terms of his national drama and his eternal questions of life ever been characterized more clearly? A poem like "I Would Like to Describe" poses three questions that every poem poses.

First, can a poet measure meaning? Second, can that measurement influence thought?

And, finally, if a poet can measure meaning, can a poet describe even the "simplest emotion" from the intimate to the political in the service of humanity?

Both Halves of a Proposition

I have never gotten over my astonishment at how a wonderful poet who was once highly regarded and highly acclaimed during his lifetime can, after his death, first recede and then slip altogether from public awareness. And then afterward, with the help of fellow poets who care deeply about the writing of the late poet—whom they feel is being slighted by contemporary fashion and literary sorting—that late poet gets a reevaluation and a new reckoning with the future.

I fear something like the wonderful-poet's-fate-of-falling-out-of-favor part has befallen the wonderful poet William Meredith, whose forty-year career as a poet began with winning the Yale Series of Younger Poets prize in 1944, and later included winning the Pulitzer Prize and the National Book Award, and other accolades such as his appointments as Chancellor of the Academy of American Poets and as the Consultant in Poetry at the Library of Congress, which we now call Poet Laureate of the United States.

Meredith's poetry has élan and intelligence and good humor. His perceptions bridge zones in the mind between consciousness and the formation of an idea. The combination of those elements, I suppose, ought to fall under the more precise term of wit. As in these lines from the ironically titled "A Major Work," which begins: "Poems are hard to read / Pictures are hard to see / Music is hard to hear / And people are hard to love."

To write with wit is to see the ways in which paradoxes have outgrown their initial insights so that both halves of a proposition feel true. An example of this intention comes in a Meredith sonnet like "The Illiterate." The poem begins with a gentle simile ("Touching your goodness, I am like a man"). But then you realize the simile is a ruse. The entire poem is an extended conceit based on dramatizing the physical and psychological consequences of not being able to touch the other person's goodness:

> Touching your goodness, I am like a man
> Who turns a letter over in his hand
> And you might think this was because the hand
> Was unfamiliar but, truth is, the man
> Has never had a letter from anyone;
> And now he is both afraid of what it means
> And ashamed because he has no other means
> To find out what it says than to ask someone.
>
> His uncle could have left the farm to him,
> Or his parents died before he sent them word,
> Or the dark girl changed and want him for beloved.
> Afraid and letter-proud, he keeps it with him.
> What would you call his feeling for the words
> That keep him rich and orphaned and beloved?

What is it one would want a new generation of poets to learn from a master like Meredith in this poem? And why should we advance his poems into the future? Because in this poem, to use it as one example, we are asked to be alert to the thrill of figuration. Figuration is the very lifeblood of poetry because it reveals the ways a mind shapes and designs ideas and feelings. Figuration is what poetry is.

Look at the end words—*man, hand, hand, man, anyone, means, means, someone, him, word, beloved, him, words, beloved.* Not only are these grouped as rhymes but they are essentially repetitions buried in the location of the rhymes, not actually rhymes themselves.

And consider what is meant by illiterate. At first glance, we are expected to think the poem might be about the inability to read. Which, in fact, it is. But not an inability to read words, though that is built into the poem's figure. Instead, it is the terribly sad inability to read the emotion of love and the inability to comprehend goodness, and then to be left abandoned in a state of fear.

In the form of an Italian sonnet, one of the art's classic fixed forms, the abstract idea of illiteracy has been made concrete. The heartbreaking emotional disqualification that Meredith exhibits here illustrates one of poetry's most urgent necessities: to be intensely wise and sensuously understanding.

Unveil the Hidden

A gray box with poetry arrived on my desk once, a gray box the color of fog in the middle of a gray night. It held photographs, ephemera, dictionary definitions, lyric shards, fragments, cutouts, clippings, handwritten jottings, and corrupted incomplete narratives. It contained bits of discarded or uncollected memories. It even had some lines of poetry in there, too.

What to make of a box like this? The pages opened like an accordion and contained the souls of the dead. Now I should say that this box also contained with all that stuff a book of poetry by Anne Carson. The box, or the book, is called *Nox*. And the book is an elegy for Carson's brother, Michael, and it also uses the Roman poet Catullus's elegy (known as Catullus 101) for his own brother as a parallel inspiration.

So *Nox*, which means night in Latin, is a box. *Nox* is a box with two dead brothers and a book inside. *Nox* is a box with two dead brothers and a dead poet and a dead language and a book inside. *Nox* is a report of death, a report to death, a letter to the self, and a memo to the muses.

The contents of *Nox* are a facsimile of a keepsake Carson made for herself after her brother Michael's death. Her elegy for him is also an attempt to translate Catullus 101 as a means both to relocate her brother's lost life and also to reformulate what it means to translate emotion into language and one language into the emotions of another language:

> Many the peoples many the oceans I crossed—
> I arrive at these poor, brother, burials
> so I could give you the last gift owed to death

and talk (why?) with mute ash.
Now that Fortune tore you from me, you
oh poor (wrongly) brother (wrongly) taken from me,
now still anyway this—what a distant mood of parents
handed down as the sad gift for burials—
accept! Soaked with tears of a brother
and into forever, brother, farewell and farewell.

I have to add this observation, too: Anne Carson is not just translating any Latin into English, or any Catullus poem. She's wrestling with Catullus 101, a poem many translators have claimed is untranslatable. While Carson cops to the struggles of translating Catullus 101, she also performs and embodies its translational potential because *Nox* enacts Catullus 101 through the act of grieving for her brother.

By doing all of that—performing, embodying, enacting, and, yes, grieving—Carson stores life into a knowable space. And that is one of the definitions of lyric poetry.

Carson then protects that space in a box as if night—or one's suffering in grief—could be contained and then shelved.

What I'm getting at is this: to translate is to unveil the hidden and *Nox* is an illustration of the impossibility of translation. It's an elegiac journey through the virtual in order to recover from an actual loss. *Nox* elegizes the elegy—because translating life into death and death back into life is the central struggle for those suffering grief.

By the time I finished reading *Nox* and finished Carson's re-formations—the way she breaks down each word of Catullus 101, one word at a time with denotative and connotative swoons and sonic hummings—I realized that only through deconstructing the material of the Catullus poem can Carson construct the meaning of her brother's life.

In the end, that's a failure. The translation can't be made. The poem can't be written. The brother can't be brought back to life. Best to accordion all those scatterings together, like a poem, inside a box.

And all of what I just said is true of writing any poem on any theme. A poem is a temporary contingency. It stands in for emotions and ideas. It stands in for rhythmic speaking. It stands in for the spoken music of language. Stands in, and stands up for.

Different Versions

My cousin once invited me to his house to show off his newly acquired framed broadside of the poem "Zenshinji" by his late friend, the poet Philip Whalen.

Whalen was born in Oregon in 1923 and grew up in The Dalles. He and my cousin attended Reed College during the Gary Snyder and Lew Welch era of the late 1940s, and lived in the same group house. A Zen monk for over thirty years and long celebrated as one of the more ascetic poets of the Beat movement, Whalen was the model for Jack Kerouac's character Warren Coughlin in *Dharma Bums*. He died in San Francisco in 2002.

Here is the poem as it reads on the broadside:

Here our days are nameless
Time all misnumbered
Right where Mr. Yeats wanted so much to be
Moving to the call of bell and semantron, rite and ceremony
Bright hard-colored tidiness, Arthur Rackham world
No soil or mulch or mud
Everything boiled and laundered and dry-cleaned
Inhabited by that race of scrubbed and polished men
Who drive the dairy trucks of San Francisco

The arts ooze forth from fractures in planes of solid rock
Outer ambition and inwards tyranny
"Hurrah for Karamazov!"
Totally insane sprung loose from all moorings
I wander about, cup of coffee in hand,
Chatting with students at work in warm spring rain

My cousin then opened the same poem in the recently published *The Collected Poems of Philip Whalen*, and pointed out the differences in the two versions. Here's the version from the book:

> Here our days are nameless time all misnumbered
> Right where Mr. Yeats wanted so much to be
> Moving to the call of bell and semantron,
>   rites and ceremonies
> Bright hard-colored tidiness Arthur Rackham world
>   (no soil or mulch or mud)
> Everything boiled and laundered and dry-cleaned
> And probably inhabited by that race of
>   scrubbed and polished men
>   who drive the dairy trucks of San Francisco
>
> The arts ooze forth from fractures in planes of solid rock
> Outer ambition and inwards tyranny
> "Hurrah for Karamazov!"
> Totally insane sprung loose from all mornings
> I wander about, cup of coffee in hand,
> Chatting with students working in warm spring rain

We began to talk about the differences. Even though neither of us were knowledgeable about the poem's textual chronology, we wanted to consider whether we thought the version of the poem on the broadside was composed first or the one in the *Collected*. Mostly we were left with curiosity about two different versions of the same poem and a lot of speculation.

At first glance the differences have to do with lineation. Lineation is the process by which a poet composes and divides up the lines in his poems. Dividing up lines is a way to stimulate new connections of ideas and emotions inside of sentences. As with nearly all of Whalen's poems—he published his first poems in the late 1940s—"Zenshinji" is composed in free verse. The line lengths are irregular and don't rest on fixed rhythms or metrical patterns.

One difference in lineation occurs in the opening lines of the broadside version where the two phrases—"Here our days are nameless" and "Time all misnumbered"—are divided into two lines. In the *Collected* version, the phrases are set into one line.

A rhythmic difference occurs in the last lines of the two versions: it's "students at work" in the broadside version and "students working" in the *Collected* version. Which one do you prefer? Depends on who you are. Reading a poem often asks you to confirm your aesthetic taste insofar as form and content go. I mean, insofar as the way you enjoy how a poet fashions form and content.

When June Jordan cracked that a bumper-sticker definition of poetry might be "Minimum Words, Maximum Content," she was making it clear that Walt Whitman's writing fit her paradigm, too, because Whitman needs all the words he uses since, after all, he's writing about the cosmos. That's all well and good unless your tastes run to something more compact, concise, and distilled like Emily Dickinson's poems. You might prefer the microscopic, not the macroscopic. But June Jordan's definition works with Dickinson, too: Emily Dickinson needs fewer words than Whitman, not because he's writing about the cosmos and she's writing about the interior rooms of her soul, but because she's studying each and every speck of her soul.

So, also, with the two "Zenshinji" versions. Reading them, you might ask yourself, what is it you like when you read a poem? What do you make of the divergent versions? How do you decide or appreciate which version is better?

I'm going to dodge discussing which version might be the more authentic. But it's worth asking, too, is *better* the right question to ask?

Hard to say. The consensus between my cousin and me was that the broadside has more immediacy and direct connection to emotion, and that we preferred it.

Whalen was often concerned with this very question of presentation and appreciation. His thoughts about his own compositional methods might provide at least one answer to some of these questions. He wrote: "I enjoy cutting and revising what I've written, for in the midst of those processes I often discover images and visions and ideas which I hadn't been conscious of before, and these add thickness and depth and solidity to the final draft, not simply polish alone."

Alertness

Richard Hugo was a rumpled, princely, softhearted poet of hard knocks. He wore his tough-guy persona like a leathery second skin. But his rough exterior hid a complicated, vulnerable inner life.

Hugo was born in 1923 in White Center, Washington, and died in 1982 after living in Missoula, Montana, for some twenty years. He was stained from a sharp blot of survival guilt from his World War II bomber runs. Read his poem "Letter to Simic from Boulder" for the full confession. His war experiences were further complicated by unkempt sadness. Anyone who has read his epistolary poems knows that there was a stretch in his life when he was terribly lonely and desperate for love.

One of the most common questions a poet fields is about how a certain poem comes into existence. For some, that's a hard question to answer. Hugo would have struggled with it. He once claimed that his poems were about "people who never were, in a place I had never been."

"Degrees of Gray in Philipsburg" is rich with this notion of coming into being. It begins:

> You might come here Sunday on a whim.
> Say your life broke down. The last good kiss
> you had was years ago. You walk these streets
> laid out by the insane, past hotels
> that didn't last, bars that did, the tortured try
> of local drivers to accelerate their lives.
> Only churches are kept up. The jail
> turned 70 this year. The only prisoner
> is always in, not knowing what he's done.

That life asserts itself in important moments "on a whim" was gospel to Hugo. The churches, the jails, and that "only prisoner" are props as much as they are characters for him in order to study the cultural and spiritual geographies of a place, a town, a landscape. What he sees in Philipsburg is bitterness:

> The principal supporting business now
> is rage. Hatred of the various grays
> the mountain sends, hatred of the mill,
> The Silver Bill repeal, the best liked girls
> who leave each year for Butte. One good
> restaurant and bars can't wipe the boredom out.
> The 1907 boom, eight going silver mines,
> a dance floor built on springs—
> all memory resolves itself in gaze,
> in panoramic green you know the cattle eat
> or two stacks high above the town,
> two dead kilns, the huge mill in collapse
> for fifty years that won't fall finally down.

It's worth noting that Hugo had a habit of driving to towns in Montana, often with a fishing pole at the ready, in order to experience those towns as his. Even though they weren't his. And then once he claimed them ("all memory resolves itself"), he would lament their "collapse."

This is a way to invent experience from experience, to invent emotion from emotion, and to find in places and towns you don't know the stories of your own life that you do:

> Isn't this your life? That ancient kiss
> still burning out your eyes? Isn't this defeat
> so accurate, the church bell simply seems
> a pure announcement: ring and no one comes?
> Don't empty houses ring? Are magnesium
> and scorn sufficient to support a town,
> not just Philipsburg, but towns
> of towering blondes, good jazz and booze
> the world will never let you have
> until the town you came from dies inside?

Say no to yourself. The old man, twenty
when the jail was built, still laughs
although his lips collapse. Someday soon,
he says, I'll go to sleep and not wake up.
You tell him no. You're talking to yourself.
The car that brought you here still runs.
The money you buy lunch with,
no matter where it's mined, is silver
and the girl who serves your food
is slender and her red hair lights the wall.

Hugo actively sought out the experiences he invents in his poems, but in the case of this poem there is an actual backstory. In his introduction to Hugo's *Collected Poems*, William Kittredge tells the story: "Annick Smith tells of traveling with her husband, David, in the spring of 1966 to film Hugo in the mining town of Philipsburg. The barren streets and the collapsing nineteenth-century silver mill were a perfect backdrop for Hugo. The footage shot that day was edited into *Kicking the Loose Gravel Home*, the film about Hugo...Hugo stayed up all that night, writing. At five in the morning he called David and Annick and read 'Degrees of Gray in Philipsburg' over the telephone."

What I adore about this anecdote is that it shows a poet at his most poet-ness. That is, alert to living one's life deeply as a precondition for writing anything like a poem.

Backbreaking

One autumn while visiting a Crook County, Oregon, mint farmer who was also a former Speaker of the House of the Oregon Legislature, I gladly followed him on a tour of his stubble fields. Wandering around together, our talk led to the necessity for successful farmers to diversify their crops. He mused out loud, "You really can't grow much in the Oregon desert."

No, you can't. And that's when I realized that a poet, too, is a diversifier.

Taking myself as a particular sort of model, I make poems, edit, give readings, lecture, write about poetry, and, for a few years there, commented on presidential politics, too.

Could it be that I'm so diversified that I could be called a literary farmer? I hope so. I love the moniker.

Robert Frost still fits the characterization of literary farmer, doesn't he? Plus, he actually farmed some property in Derry, New Hampshire, during the first decade of the twentieth century. His literary crop was diversified with teaching, writing, giving readings, and lecturing. In addition to tending to sonnets, monologues, and lyric poems while living in Derry, Frost managed poultry, a scattering of fruit trees, a small hay field, a kitchen garden, and a decent-sized stand of maple trees for sugaring. It was on that New Hampshire farm that Frost wrote some of his most beloved poems, including "Home Burial," "My November Guest," "Death of the Hired Man," and many other poems in his first two books, *A Boy's Will* and *North of Boston*.

"Putting in the Seed," published in 1916 in his third book, *Mountain Interval*, was likely inspired by the intricate, intimate relationship between time and landscape so prevalent in farm life:

> You come to fetch me from my work to-night
> When supper's on the table, and we'll see
> If I can leave off burying the white
> Soft petals fallen from the apple tree.
> (Soft petals, yes, but not so barren quite,
> Mingled with these, smooth bean and wrinkled pea;)
> And go along with you ere you lose sight
> Of what you came for and become like me,
> Slave to a springtime passion for the earth.
> How Love burns through the Putting in the Seed
> On through the watching for that early birth
> When, just as the soil tarnishes with weed,
> The sturdy seedling with arched body comes
> Shouldering its way and shedding the earth crumbs.

Is it safe to assume that the poems Frost wrote in Derry and afterwards have something of his difficult marriage to Elinor White, too? Perhaps. Something of the management of the, well, crops of eros seems present in the poem from the "soft petals fallen" to the "springtime passion" and finally to the erotic image of the "arched body."

Keep this fact in mind, too. By the time the Frosts had arrived in Derry, they had already lost their eldest son. By the time they moved away from the farm around 1909, another child, an infant daughter, had also died.

"Putting in the Seed" is fraught with a mixture of stubborn and untilled emotions and circumstances.

Farm life, lived life, aesthetic life: from a field of complex emotions, from a pivot of metaphor, from the sunrise to sunset ethic of laboring over each stress and syllable of language, a poet digs into experience, seeds meaning, awaits inspiration, and gets to work. It's backbreaking—in its fashion.

Frame of Reference

When twenty-one-year-old Army combat medic Don Unrau arrived in Vietnam in June 1971, only to be flown out six months later with a land mine wound to his stomach, he figured he'd never be back.

But watching televised broadcasts of the Gulf War in Iraq twenty years later in 1991 stirred something in the photographer he'd become after taking advantage of the GI Bill. Looking to revise what Vietnam meant to him, he decided to return in the early 1990s to take pictures. Then he returned for several subsequent years, even before US-Vietnamese normalization.

You can find his riveting photographs from these excursions in his book, *Spring Visits*, published by Stray Dog Press. In portraits, landscapes, and snapshots, a figurative banality underscores the emotional weight with images of village roads, opera houses, the Ha Noi intersection with bicycles and scooters, and a corner KFC. Whether it's a picture of a tennis lesson or a badminton court, the images redefine, for the photographer at least, that human beings always seek out normalcy during and, surely, in the aftermath of a violent crisis like war.

There are reminders of the war in the photographs, of course—a man resting on forgotten bomb casings in front of a ticket office in Vinh Moc, a bomb crater in a field near Xuan Loc, and a museum at My Lai. But the book is more a quiet evocation of daily life than a singular reevaluation of post-war Vietnam from the eyes of a returning American vet.

Unrau is drawn instead to the the physical pleasures of living. He slyly reveals a calm geography that undercuts my American expectation of photographic irony or documentary tension. Instead, I'm asked to witness a morning's labors along a riverside, a small girl in a white dress, lovers on a motorcycle near White Silk Lake, two teenagers having a foot race in the park in Ho Chi Minh City, merchants selling wares from the aisle of a train.

The book is prefaced with a poem, "Spring-Watching Pavilion," by the eighteenth-century Vietnamese poet Ho Xuan Huong, whose poems were politically irreverent and sexually allusive:

> A gentle spring evening arrives
> airily, unclouded by worldly dust.
>
> Three times the bell tolls echoes like a wave.
> We see heaven upside-down in sad puddles.
>
> Love's vast sea cannot be emptied.
> And springs of grace flow easily everywhere.
>
> Where is nirvana?
> Nirvana is here, nine times out of ten.

As rendered in John Balaban's translations, Ho Xuan Huong's poems shimmer with wit and earthiness—much like Unrau's photographs. From the arrival of an "unclouded" evening to the sound of bells tolling, from love's vast fullness to the omnipresence of heaven, the poem acts as a snapshot of timelessness, of ordinariness, and of valiant calm.

I've begun to wonder, more so than usual, about the role a single poem can play in the imagination of a single reader. For Unrau, Ho's poem, composed hundreds of years before he began his photographic journey in her homeland, seemed to connect her heart to his frame of reference.

Not surprisingly, but still a little strangely, we poets expect our readers to read poems the way we do: book by book. But most readers don't read this way. Yet it's been my faith that most people have a single poem that means something important to them. That seems to have been the case with Don Unrau, who found himself reading "Spring-Watching Pavilion" in a way that makes it essential to him and his experience: as a single poem in relation to his own life, and as a poem that he can incorporate into how he views, and even revises, one of the crucial and defining eras of both his early life and the nation's history.

Unacknowledged Laws

One question I wrestle with often is, can poetry catalyze a more civilized political engagement?

The partisan warfare in any country is both real and, typically, ill-mannered. Mockery and vilification are preeminent, with language used as a weapon of thrust and parry. And, yes, while both poetry and politics share an interest in rhetoric, the former is for transformation, while the latter is for persuasion, sometimes for manipulation, certainly for power.

At its worst, in politics it's not enough to question the ideas of the other. Your opponent's motives must be suspect or amoral. Soapbox conservatives tag liberals as bloodless elites while bullhorn liberals call out conservatives for being racist buffoons. To both, I say bunk.

What might poetry do? It's not that the center cannot hold, as W. B. Yeats once feared. It's that the center is silenced. Inflammatory words dominate our political discourse. Reasoned thought based on human experience has been banished in a tribalistic contest of left and right.

If poets, as Percy Shelley says, are the unacknowledged legislators of the world, then might poems be our unacknowledged laws? What is the future of our patchwork democracy if language is just a nasty weapon for continual partisan wrestling?

In answer to these questions, a poem: Wilfred Owen's "Strange Meeting," which captures a sudden encounter in the afterlife by two soldiers who had killed each other in battle the day before. It begins:

> It seemed that out of battle I escaped
> Down some profound dull tunnel, long since scooped
> Through granites which titanic wars had groined.

From dullness comes pain and distress, and the entrance to Hell:

> Yet also there encumbered sleepers groaned,
> Too fast in thought or death to be bestirred.
> Then, as I probed them, one sprang up, and stared
> With piteous recognition in fixed eyes,
> Lifting distressful hands, as if to bless.
> And by his smile, I knew that sullen hall,—
> By his dead smile I knew we stood in Hell.

Owen is presenting an argument about the necessity to survive in combat, about the need to redeem one's patriotism, but also the recognition that both necessity and need are futile.

The ensuing dialogue brings the burden of warfare to its crisis:

> With a thousand fears that vision's face was grained;
> Yet no blood reached there from the upper ground,
> And no guns thumped, or down the flues made moan.
> "Strange friend," I said, "here is no cause to mourn."
> "None," said that other, "save the undone years,
> The hopelessness. Whatever hope is yours,
> Was my life also; I went hunting wild
> After the wildest beauty in the world,
> Which lies not calm in eyes, or braided hair,
> But mocks the steady running of the hour,
> And if it grieves, grieves richlier than here.
> For of my glee might many men have laughed,
> And of my weeping something had been left,
> Which must die now. I mean the truth untold,
> The pity of war, the pity war distilled.
> Now men will go content with what we spoiled,
> Or, discontent, boil bloody, and be spilled.
> They will be swift with swiftness of the tigress.
> None will break ranks, though nations trek from progress.
> Courage was mine, and I had mystery,
> Wisdom was mine, and I had mastery:
> To miss the march of this retreating world
> Into vain citadels that are not walled.
> Then, when much blood had clogged their chariot-wheels,

I would go up and wash them from sweet wells,
Even with truths that lie too deep for taint.
I would have poured my spirit without stint
But not through wounds; not on the cess of war.
Foreheads of men have bled where no wounds were.
I am the enemy you killed, my friend.
I knew you in this dark: for so you frowned
Yesterday through me as you jabbed and killed.
I parried; but my hands were loath and cold.
Let us sleep now. . . . "

The rhyming couplets of this poem echo the rhyming couplets of partisanship. Left, right. Liberal, conservative. Progress, restraint. Pair after pair reinforces the mind of the poem: *moan, mourn; laughed, left; mystery, mastery; killed, cold.*

A poem like "Strange Meeting" argues that we destroy our mutual spirit, competitive generosity, and republic of thought whenever we treat those whose ideas differ from ours as venal or vicious. Poetry identifies the futility of this behavior and reinforces the commonality in our shared experience.

Rex the Rocking Horse and Sammy the Seal

When my son was small and I could still put him to bed by reading to him, he had an expression that, in its fashion, wonderfully captured the essence of our human need both to tell and to listen to stories.

Curious George over, *The Roly-Poly Pudding* over, *Abiyoyo* over, he would try to keep the intimacy of the bedtime ritual going by asking, "Will you tell me a story without a book?"

So I'd settle onto his bed a bit longer and conjure up the characters we had invented together. These included two small brass figures that sat on a shelf in the living room of our house and which, according to the legends we invented, came to real life when the house was empty. Of the adventures of Rex the Rocking Horse and Sammy the Seal, the one recurring detail was that both figures deeply longed to be a little boy. They also never wanted the actual little boy living in the house to catch them in their exploits. So whenever he appeared, which he always did, they would quickly hop up onto the shelf and magically become brass animals again.

Our brass heroes were both a mirror and a window for my son's own curiosities about the mysterious interior recesses of the self.

The need to listen to the sound of another person's voice in the act of delighting in—you name it, gossip, tale, legend, anecdote, chronicle, yarn, or bedtime story—is just as great and necessary as the mysterious urge to tell the stories in the first place.

Our instinct for language, our desire to sing for the sake of the song, and our sharing of what lies in one's heart is at the root of human consciousness. It's the footprint for our human commonality—the very act of storytelling, I mean—and that footprint is rooted in the vowels and consonants of a common language and in the beats and rhythms of common speech.

The footprint, also, is wound up with poetry's most urgent lyric calling: to make language feel and sound so exceptional that it's like music.

I was reminded one time by the poet Kevin Craft that music is the pure speech of the Muses ("muse" from the Greek "mousa," meaning something like all creative activity). He meant, I suppose, that the Muses literally speak in music. This ideal is precisely what poets strive to achieve. We strive to discover and reveal the deepest delight where music and language mingle. It's not just that a muse inspires a poet, but the poet tries to keep the conversation going in an utterance of music that her muse will understand.

Something of that urge toward "deep delight" draws me to lines of a poem called "Tell Me a Story" by the wonderful American poet Robert Penn Warren. I wonder these days why Warren is not a poet younger poets read; he's so lyrically agile and his commitment to expressing the large themes of literature is vast. "Tell Me a Story" is the final poem in a powerful sequence Warren published in 1969 called *Audubon: A Vision.* Here is part one:

> Long ago, in Kentucky, I, a boy, stood
> By a dirt road, in first dark, and heard
> The great geese hoot northward.
>
> I could not see them, there being no moon
> And the stars sparse. I heard them.
>
> I did not know what was happening in my heart.
>
> It was the season before the elderberry blooms,
> Therefore they were going north.
>
> The sound was passing northward.

The poem captures the visceral, inexplicable sway of poetry. The second part of the poem concludes:

Tell me a story.

In this century, and moment, of mania,
Tell me a story.

Make it a story of great distances, and starlight.

The name of the story will be Time,
But you must not pronounce its name.

Tell me a story of deep delight.

This line—"I did not know what was happening in my heart"—is one of my favorite lines in the poem. It dramatizes the poet's realization that the shared experience of both telling and hearing stories can stimulate.

It dramatizes the reader's experience, too. As with the metaphor of Rex and Sammy in their quest to become a human boy, the mysterious interior recesses of the self are the passages through time and space that poems aspire to locate. Call them epic, dramatic, lyric, or narrative. The results are, one and all, poetry.

No human culture we know of has existed without poetry. We turn to poems when we fall in love and when we break up, when we send soldiers to war and when we bury them. We turn to poetry during every passage of our existence. We turn to poetry to mythologize our life-forming, life-changing, and life-affirming experiences.

Poetry is life. Without it, we'd be less human. With it, we are invited to understand more fully our fate and our feelings in the world.

Reading List

Akhmatova, Anna (1976). *Selected Poems*. Trans. by D. M. Thomas. Penguin.

Allison, Alexander W. et al., eds. (1983). *The Norton Anthology of Poetry*.

American Poetry: The Twentieth Century (2000). 2 vols. Library of America.

Ammons, A. R. (1983). *Lake Country Effect*. W. W. Norton.

Andrade, Eugenio de (2003). *Forbidden Words. Selected Poetry*. Trans. by Alexis Levitan. New Directions.

Ansel, Talvikki (2003). *The Jetty & Other Poems*. Zoo Press.

Barnstone, Tony and Chou Ping, eds. (2005). *The Anchor Book of Chinese Poetry*. Anchor Books.

Bierds, Linda (2002). *The Seconds*. Putnam.

Bishop, Elizabeth (1983). *Complete Poems: 1927–1979*. Farrar, Straus and Giroux.

Bloom, Harold, ed. (2006). *American Religious Poems*. Library of America.

Brown, Kurt and Harold Shechter, eds. (2008). *Conversation Pieces. Poems That Talk to Other Poems*. Alfred A. Knopf.

Carson, Ann (2010). *Nox*. New Directions.

Christensen, Inger (2004). *Butterfly Valley. A Requiem*. Trans. by Susanna Nied. New Directions.

Collier, Michael (2006). *Dark Wild Realm*. Houghton Mifflin.

Cope, Wendy (1986). *Making Cocoa for Kingsley Amis*. Faber & Faber.

Di Piero, W. S. (2004). *Brother Fire*. Alfred A. Knopf.

Dickinson, Emily (1976). *Complete Poems*. Ed. by Thomas H. Johnson. Back Bay Books.

Frost, Robert (1949). *Complete Poems*. Holt, Rinehart, and Winston.

Ginsberg, Allen (2001). *Howl and Other Poems*. City Lights Books.

Glück, Louise (2006). *Averno*. Farrar, Straus and Giroux.

Gunn, Thom (1992). *The Man with Night Sweats*. Farrar, Straus and Giroux.

Heaney, Seamus (2006). *District and Circle*. Farrar, Straus and Giroux.

Hecht, Anthony (1990). *Collected Earlier Poems*. Alfred A. Knopf.

Hensley, Jeannine, ed. (1981). *The Works of Anne Bradstreet*. Belknap Press.

Herbert, George (2004). *The Complete English Poems*. Ed. by John Tobin. Penguin.

Herbert, Zbigniew (1968). *Selected Poems*. Trans. by Czeslaw Milosz and Peter Dale Scott. Penguin.

Hughes, Ted (2003). *Collected Poems*. Farrar, Straus and Giroux.

Hugo, Richard (1991). *Making Certain It Goes On. The Collected Poems*. W. W. Norton.

Huong, Ho Xuan (2000). *Spring-Watching Pavilion*. Trans. by John Balaban. Copper Canyon Press.

Jones, Rodney (1996). *Things That Happen Once*. Houghton Mifflin.

Justice, Donald (2004). *Collected Poems*. Alfred A. Knopf.

Keats, John (1958). *Selected Poems and Letters*. Ed. by Douglas Bush. Riverside Editions.

Keegan, Paul, ed. (2000). *The New Penguin Book of English Verse*. Penguin.

Kenney, Richard (2008). *The One-Strand River*. Alfred A. Knopf.

Kleinzahler, August (2003). *The Strange Hours Travelers Keep*. Farrar, Straus and Giroux.

Kunitz, Stanley (2000). *The Collected Poems*. W. W. Norton.

Larkin, Philip (1989). *Collected Poems*. Farrar, Straus and Giroux.

Levertov, Denise (2002). *Selected Poems*. New Directions.

Levin, Phyllis (2008). *May Day*. Penguin.

Lowell, Robert (2003). *Collected Poems*. Farrar, Straus and Giroux.

Lucie-Smith, Edward, ed. (1967). *The Penguin Book of Satiric Verse*. Penguin.

Mandelstam, Osip (1981). *Stone*. Trans. by Robert Tracy. Harvill Books.

Matthews, William (1989). *Blues If You Want*. Houghton Mifflin.

Meredith, William (1997). *Effort at Speech. New and Selected Poems*. TriQuarterly / Northwestern University Press.

Milton, John (2004). *Complete Poems*. Penguin.

Neruda, Pablo (1993). *Twenty Love Poems and a Song of Despair*. Trans. by W. S. Merwin. Penguin.

Ovid's Poetry of Exile (1990). Trans. by David R. Slavitt. Johns Hopkins University Press.

Pinsky, Robert, ed. (2009). *Essential Pleasures. A New Anthology of Poems to Read Aloud.* W. W. Norton.

Plumly, Stanley (2007). *Old Heart.* W. W. Norton.

Pope, Alexander (1978). *Poetical Works.* Ed. by Herbert Davis and Pat Rogers. Oxford University Press.

Rich, Adrienne (2004). *The School Among the Ruins. Poems 2000–2004.* W. W. Norton.

Rukeyser, Muriel (2004). *Selected Poems.* Ed. by Adrienne Rich. Library of America.

Shapiro, Harvey, ed. (2003). *Poets of World War II.* Library of America.

Sidney, Philip (2009). *The Major Works.* Ed. by Katherine Duncan-Jones. Oxford University Press.

Stallings, A. E. (2012). *Olives.* Northwestern University Press.

Stevens, Wallace (1990). *The Collected Poems.* Vintage.

Stevenson, Anne (2002). *Selected Poems.* Library of America.

Thomas, Dylan (1952). *Selected Poems: 1934–1952.* New Directions.

Thomas, Harry, ed. (2005). *Montale in English.* Handsel Books.

Tranströmer, Tomas (2006). *The Great Enigma. New Collected Poems.* Trans. by Robin Fulton. New Directions.

Trethewey, Natasha (2006). *Native Guard.* Houghton Mifflin.

Vallejo, Cesar (2003). *The Black Heralds.* Trans. by Rebecca Seiferle. Copper Canyon Press.

Warn, Emily (2008). *Shadow Architect.* Copper Canyon Press.

Warren, Robert Penn (1969). *Audubon. A Vision.* Random House.

Whalen, Philip (2008). *The Collected Poems.* Ed. by Michael Rothenberg. Wesleyan University Press.

Whitman, Walt (1973). *Leaves of Grass.* W. W. Norton.

Wilbur, Richard (2004). *Collected Poems, 1943–2004.* Harcourt Inc.

Williams, C. K. (2006). *Collected Poems.* Farrar, Straus and Giroux.

Williams, Oscar, ed. (1947). *A Little Treasury of Great Poetry.* Scribner's.

Wiman, Christian (2005). *Hard Night.* Copper Canyon Press.

Wordsworth, William (1995). *Poems.* Everyman's Library.

Wright, Charles (2002). *A Short History of the Shadow.* Farrar, Straus and Giroux.

Yeats, W. B. (1967). *The Collected Poems.* Macmillan.

Zagajewski, Adam (2008). *Eternal Enemies.* Trans. by Claire Cavanaugh. Farrar, Straus and Giroux.

Acknowledgments

As Christopher Hitchens says, the "thanking of friends, colleagues, and co-conspirators ought to be the most enjoyable part of the completion of any work. However, the accumulation of decades of debt now forces a choice between the invidious and the ingratiating." So rather than rattle off one of those embarrassing catalogs of names, I'm going to aim for something briefer and limit my gratitudes to those associated with the writing of these individual ruminations. To everyone else (you know who you are) my deepest thanks.

Various parts of "Thrill at the Triumphs" originally appeared in *The Rumpus* and on the Poetry Foundation's website. My appreciation to editors Brian Spears and Emily Warn, respectively.

Other passages of "Thrill at the Triumphs" and all the other pieces in this book were first published, in one form or another, in the *Oregonian*. The titles of each essay presented here have been designed exclusively for this collection. At the *Oregonian* I owe a big thanks to Peggy McMullen and especially to Jeff Baker, a true friend of the poets, for commissioning and editing my writing for a decade. Both made a valiant effort to make me a better typist of the lines of poetry I typed for quotations for the pieces—a valiant effort that has, alas, failed, because I'm all thumbs in this regard—and I'm eternally grateful. On behalf of the poets whose lines I flubbed and that Peggy and Jeff corrected, thanks to them for rooting out my errors.

I also wish to thank Don Selby and Diane Boller at *Poetry Daily*, Rus Bowden at *Poetry and Poets in Rags*, and Ron Silliman of *Silliman's Blog*, for graciously reposting online links to earlier versions of these pieces, and to many other blogs and online venues, too many to name, for the same.

And to the editors at Antilever Press for good sense, wise counsel, and friendship, plus my immense appreciation for their advocacy of poetry criticism.

I'm thankful to Jennifer Urban, Director of the Samuelson Law, Technology, and Public Policy Clinic at the University of California at Berkeley School of Law, as well as clinical students Tiffany Martin and Musetta Durkee, for their time and advice in the area of fair use law in the United States. Great thanks, too, to Dana Gioia, Jonathan Galassi, and Jeff Shotts for suggestions and advice, to Holly Roland for editorial assistance, and to the Lannan Foundation for providing a retreat in West Texas.

Gratitude, also, to the many, many students of mine whose questions and insights inspired some of these pieces, as well as to friends and fellow poets for the same reason. And especially to my teachers. I hope I have paid an honor to them here for what I have learned and continue to learn from their poems, their ideas about poetry, and their friendship. Acknowledgments also to the many poets and publishing houses that generously and voluntarily sent me so many new books of poetry every year in the hope that something might pique my interest to write about.

Finally, I'm grateful to the last for the seriously fascinating inspiration I get from the full catastrophe of my family and our home in Portland, and to my wife, Wendy, for creating our life of poetry as life.

DB

CPSIA information can be obtained
at www.ICGtesting.com
Printed in the USA
FSOW01n0248141015
12130FS